FRESH CUT
SUE SPARGO

A Note From Sue:

For Fresh Cut I used a selection of my favorite stitches and threads which I encourage you to try, as they really add texture and depth to your blocks.

You will refer to the photographs and diagrams in this book for stitch placement and then to my book 'Creative Stitching Second Edition' for embroidery stitch instruction. Stitches listed in 'Fresh Cut' are in bold, followed by the page number reference for detailed stitch instruction found in 'Creative Stitching Second Edition'.

'Creative Stitching' is a fantastic stitcher's resource. Along with having in depth, detailed stitch instructions and illustrations, it includes a chapter on needles and threads. I encourage you to read through this section as it is a great reference guide with regards to thread and needle compatibility.

To differentiate between the varying weights of Eleganza thread, the spools center cores are different colors, conveniently this color coding translates to the labels on my brand of needles; (i.e.) 8wt Perle Cottons are wound on green spools and should be used with a #3 Milliners (needle tube labeled with a green sticker):

Green for weight 8 (#8)
Purple for weight 5 (#5)
Turquoise for weight 3 (#3)

Note: You will use a #24 Chenille needle for stitching unless otherwise stated in the stitch directions.

If you don't have a good needle roll to organize your needles in, I'd suggest you look into making one! I have a great one in pattern and kit form available through my website!

The Roadrunner Needle Roll

© Sue Spargo 2018. This book and quilt design is protected by Federal Copyright Law together with the photographs, images and text. Neither this product nor any part of this product may be reproduced in any form unless otherwise stated, including photocopying without the expressed written consent of Sue Spargo. You may use this pattern to make a quilt for your personal use and also to make quilts for nonprofit groups as long as you give me credit as the pattern source. You may not make quilts in these patterns to sell. I encourage you to teach classes in this design as long as you require each student to buy their own copy of this book. All rights reserved.

TABLE OF CONTENTS

Supply List	2
Block 1	5
Block 2	13
Block 3	23
Block 4	31
Block 5	37
Block 6	43
Block 7	51
Block 8	59
Block 9	67
Block 10	75
Block 11	83
Block Assembly	93
Borders	96
Finishing	98
English Garden Needle Roll	100
The Fresh Cut Sewing Box	110
Stitch Key	117

SUPPLY LIST

Backgrounds:

Hand Dyed Wool:

Solid Black Wool • 1 yard
Check Black Wool • ½ yard
Plaid Black Wool • ½ yard
Textured Black Wool • Fat ¼
Striped Black Wool • 16" x 6-½"

Solid Black Wool (Border) • Long ½ yard (16" x 48")

Layering Ribbons:

¾" wide Black Alphabet Ribbon • 3-½"
⅜" wide Black with White Dot • 5"
⅜" wide Black Swiss Dot • 5-½"
½" wide Black Rick Rack • 10"

Layering Fabrics:

Fat ⅛th
Black Grunge
Black Mini Polka Dot
Black Dash
Soft Grey Texture
Black Australian Words
Black Floral Words

Fat 1/16th
Hill Dash on Black
Black Small Polka Dot
White Sphere on Black
Large White Dot on Black
Bees on Black
Black Silver Metallic

Fat 1/32nd
Black Denim
Grey Silver Metallic
Smoke Silk
Black Essex
Black Gold Metallic

Wool Appliqué:

Fat ⅛th
Cloud
Pumpkin
Spring Leaf

Fat 1/16th
Amazon Green
Blue Iris
Electric Lime
Kumquat
Lagoon
Lavender
Oceanfront

Fat 1/32nd
Artichoke Heart
Dogwood Rose
Flamingo
Goldenrod
Holly Berry
Mango
Peridot
Pine Needle
Powder Blue
Rhubarb
Turquoise

Fat 1/64th
Avocado
Baby Blue
Blue Spruce
Creamed Butter
Crystal Blue
Dark Cerise
Deep Teal
Eggplant
Flame
Larkspur
Old Gold
Orchid
Persimmon
Primrose
Raspberry
Salmon
Sea Spray
Sun Yellow
Very Berry

Additional Appliqué:

Cotton Fabrics:

20" x 5"
White Dot on Blue

10" x 4"
Avocado Grunge
Artichoke Heart Crackle
Solid Lime Green
Blue Stripe
Green Scallop
Aqua with Button Flowers

8" x 8"
Artichoke Heart Texture
Red Lotus Leaf
Green Stripe
Purple Ferns
Green Oriental Trees

6" x 6"
White Square on Flame
Turquoise Crosses on Green
Orange Dot
Yellow Ribbon Stripe
Red Grunge
Green with Pins
Purple Stripe
Rainbow Swirl
Sea Spray Grunge
Blue Teardrop
Turquoise Square on Yellow
Cream Line
Yellow Dot on Mustard
Winter Strata Stripes
Birds and Flowers on Orange
Turquoise and White Leaves on Spring Leaf
White Crosses on Avocado
Wine Pods
Green Paperweights on Black
Black with Button Flowers
Green Triangles
Cloud Roman Glass

Velvet:

Cherry • 8" x 2"
Beetroot • 3" x 3"
Oriental Poppy • 3" x 1-½"
Blue Spruce Silk • 4" x 3"
Presto Sheer • 3" x 3"

Ribbons:

⅜" wide Aqua Green Stems • 2-½"
⅝" wide Blue Flower Wheel on Green • 3"
⅜" wide Mint and Mustard Stems • 3-½"
⅜" wide Green Fanciful Stripes • 5"
⅜" wide Lime Green Purple Arrows • 7"
³⁄₁₆" wide Avocado Rick Rack • 13"
⁵⁄₁₆" wide Spring Leaf Rick Rack • 16"
¼" wide Artichoke Heart Rick Rack • 6-½"
⁵⁄₁₆" wide Lagoon Rick Rack • 24"
¼" wide Lavender Rick Rack • 4"
Painter's Thread Ribbon Floss Cotton Tape Klimt • 18"
Painter's Thread Ribbon Floss Cotton Tape Turner • 18"

Other:

⁵⁄₁₆" wide Black Buttons • 7pc

Finishing:

Backing:

Cotton Fabric • 1-⅝ yard
Insert Strip • 20" x 1-⅝ yard
White Cotton Fabric for Label • 8" square

Binding:

White Dot on Black • ½ yard

Appliqué Threads:

Ellana Wool Thread:

- EN07 Oceanfront
- EN08 Turquoise
- EN09 Amazon Green
- EN10 Spring Leaf
- EN11 Artichoke Heart
- EN12 Avocado
- EN13 Electric Lime
- EN14 Peridot
- EN16 Pine Needle
- EN17 Blue Spruce
- EN18 Lagoon
- EN19 Sea Spray
- EN20 Cloud
- EN21 Rhubarb
- EN22 Raspberry
- EN23 Flamingo
- EN24 Primrose
- EN25 Salmon
- EN31 Creamed Butter
- EN33 Goldenrod
- EN34 Sun Yellow
- EN35 Old Gold
- EN36 Orchid
- EN37 Very Berry
- EN39 Eggplant
- EN40 Blue Iris
- EN41 Flame
- EN42 Holly Berry
- EN43 Dark Cerise
- EN46 Mango
- EN47 Pumpkin
- EN48 Persimmon
- EN49 Kumquat
- EN53 Baby Blue
- EN54 Powder Blue
- EN56 Crystal Blue
- EN57 Larkspur
- EN58 Lavender
- EN59 Dogwood Rose
- EN60 Deep Teal

Efina Cotton Thread:

- EF02 Latte
- EF04 Grey Flannel
- EF06 Charcoal
- EF08 Turquoise
- EF10 Spring Leaf
- EF11 Artichoke Heart
- EF12 Avocado
- EF14 Peridot
- EF16 Pine Needle
- EF17 Blue Spruce
- EF18 Lagoon
- EF19 Sea Spray
- EF20 Cloud
- EF25 Salmon
- EF30 Black
- EF34 Sun Yellow
- EF35 Old Gold
- EF36 Orchid
- EF41 Flame
- EF43 Dark Cerise
- EF47 Pumpkin
- EF49 Kumquat
- EF54 Powder Blue
- EF58 Lavender

Embellishment Threads:

#8 Eleganza Perle Cotton:

- EZ04 Manatee
- EZ51 Purple Sortie Cap
- EZM04 Carbon
- EZM12 Inchworm
- EZM14 Lettuce Wrap
- EZM19 Island Oasis
- EZM25 Clambake
- EZM36 Plush Lilac
- EZM81 Victory Bell
- EZM95 Battlefield
- EZM99 Treasure Your Chest (BCA)

#5 Eleganza Perle Cotton:

- EZ06 Snow Globe
- EZ11 Heavy Skies
- EZ52 Love-Lies-Bleeding
- EZM31 Hibiscus
- EZM82 Haymaker's Punch
- EZM87 Heard it Through the Grapevine
- EZM93 Marsh Grass
- EZM97 Navy Jack
- EZM100 Pinking up the Pieces (BCA)
- EZM102 Current

#3 Eleganza Perle Cotton:

- EZ30 After Dinner Mint
- EZM07 Bee Pollen
- EZM13 Over the Clover
- EZM101 Fight Like a Girl (BCA)

Razzle:

- RZ3130 Aqua Sea
- RZM19 Pink Warrior (BCA)

Dazzle:

- DZ1113 Survivor (BCA)

Other:

- **Painter's Thread #3** Grandma Moses
- **The Thread Gatherer 4mm Silk Ribbon** Pond Scum
- **The Thread Gatherer Silken Pearl** Tuscan Sun
- **Painter's Thread Soft Cotton** Rousseau
- **Petite Very Velvet** Green (V621)
- **Gold Rush 14** Purple (216C)

Block 1
Finished Size: 10" x 13" + ¼" Seam Allowance

Appliqué Threads:

Ellana Wool Thread:
EN07 Oceanfront
EN13 Electric Lime
EN18 Lagoon
EN37 Very Berry
EN39 Eggplant
EN41 Flame
EN46 Mango

Efina Cotton Thread:
EF06 Charcoal
EF10 Spring Leaf
EF14 Peridot
EF25 Salmon
EF30 Black
EF41 Flame
EF54 Powder Blue

Embellishment Threads:

Eleganza Perle Cotton:
#8 EZM04 Carbon
#8 EZM12 Inchworm
#8 EZM19 Island Oasis
#3 EZ30 After Dinner Mint

Special Edition Breast Cancer Awareness Collection:
#8 EZM99 Treasure your Chest
#5 EZM100 Pinking up the Pieces
#3 EZM101 Fight Like a Girl
Razzle RZM19 Pink Warrior
Dazzle DZ1113 Survivor

Background Fabrics:

Hand Dyed Wool:
Plaid Black Wool
Solid Black Wool

Cottons & More:
Black Denim
Black Floral Words
Black Small Polka Dot

Appliqué:

Hand Dyed Wool:
Eggplant
Electric Lime
Flame
Lagoon
Mango
Oceanfront
Very Berry

Cottons & More:
Solid Lime Green
Blue Tear Drop
Green Stripe
Red Lotus Leaf
Oriental Poppy Hand Dyed Velvet
³⁄₁₆" wide Avocado Rick Rack

Background Assembly:

Background:

Cut: Plaid Black Wool - 10-½" x 8"
Solid Black Wool - 10-½" x 6"

Sew together using a ¼" seam allowance and press the seams open.

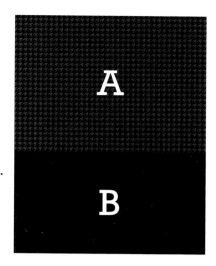

Background Layering:

Cut: Black Floral Words Cotton - 5-½" x 2-½"
Black Denim - 2" x 6-½"
Black Small Polka Dot Cotton - 1-½" x 1-½" (Cut 3)

Using the photograph provided on page 5, appliqué the layering pieces to the background.

Appliqué:

Stem:

Cut the Solid Lime Green stem ¾" x 5-¼" for needle turn. If you are making your stem using a ¼" bias maker, cut the stem ½" x 5-¼". Referring to the photograph on page 5, pin and appliqué the stem to the background.

Flower Center:

For the 1" Very Berry circle, you can either use a freezer paper template or our 1" wool punch. Place at the top of the stem and appliqué in place.

Base of Leaves, Flowers and Vase:

Trace separately with a pencil on the matte side of your freezer paper the base elements for the leaves, flowers and vase. Cut out each of the freezer paper templates on the pencil line. Referring to the photograph, iron the templates to the appropriate color wool and cotton fabrics. The shiny side of your freezer paper is ironed to the right side of all your fabrics. Cut out the wool appliqué pieces to the exact size of the templates. For the cotton fabrics, add a ¼" seam allowance so you can needle turn these fabrics. Using your small appliqué pins, pin and appliqué the rick rack stem and all the base images in place. Make sure the rick rack stem tucks under the vase and small flower.

Layering of Leaves, Flowers and Vase:

For the layering of the leaves, flowers and vase; cut templates out of freezer paper. Referring to the photograph, iron the templates to the appropriate color wool and cotton fabrics. Cut out the wool appliqué pieces to the exact size of the template. For the cotton fabrics add a ¼" seam allowance so you can needle turn the fabrics. For the vase, use a ½" wool punch to create nine

½" circles from the Very Berry wool. Appliqué the layering to the leaves, flowers and vase.

Velvet Circles:

For the two Oriental Poppy velvet circles on the Oceanfront wool flower, trace two ½" circles on your freezer paper. Cut them out on the line and iron to the wrong side of the velvet. I use a circle template to do these. Adding a ¼" seam allowance, cut out each velvet circle. In the seam allowance, stitch a small basting stitch with a contrasting color cotton thread around each circle. Draw the basting thread up so that the seam allowance pulls up around the freezer paper. Appliqué the two velvet circles in place. After stitching ¾ of the way around each of the circles, remove the basting thread and freezer paper with tweezers and complete the stitching.

Embellish:

Background:

▶ Using #8 EZM04, stitch **Cross Stitches** in the black denim rectangle.

Large Center Flower:

▶ Draw chalk lines for all the couched lines from the center of the flower to the 3 Oceanfront triangles and the four Flame ovals.

Stems:

▶ Using #3 EZ30 with a #18 Chenille needle as the thread to lay down and #8 EZM19 as the thread to stitch, **Couch** (page 45) on all the chalk lines.

Oceanfront Triangles:

▶ Using #8 EZM19, stitch a **Backstitch** (page 34) around the Oceanfront triangles and three vertical lines through each flower.
▶ Using a #15 Milliners needle and #3 EZM101, stitch three **Pistil Stitches** (page 106) at the base of each triangle.

Flame Ovals:

▶ Using #8 EZM99, stitch a **Fly Stitch** (page 127) around each oval.

Large Petals:

▶ Using #5 EZM100, stitch a **Backstitch** (page 34) around each petal.
▶ Using a #3 Milliners needle and #8 EZM19, stitch **Bullion Knots** (page 92) around the Mango wool layers of the petals.

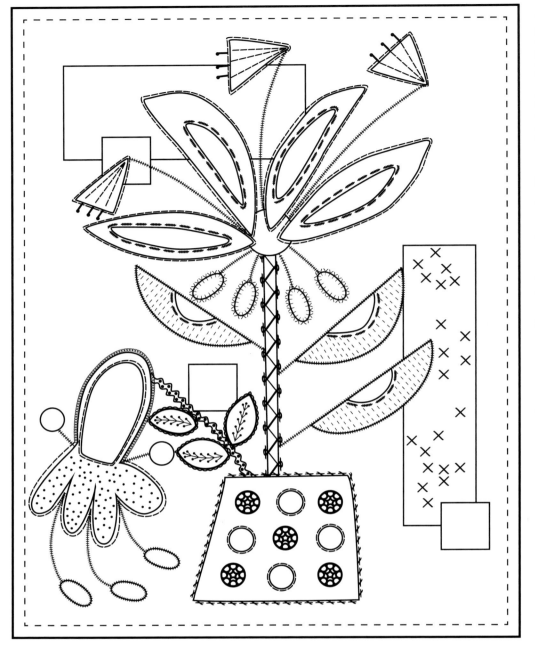

Stems:

► Using a #3 Milliners needle and #8 EZM12, stitch **French Knots** (page 104) with two wraps on each hill of the rick rack stem.
► Using #8 EZM12, stitch a **Herringbone Stitch** (page 168) over the Solid Lime Green stem.

Three Large Leaves:

► Using #3 EZ30 with a #18 Chenille needle as the thread to lay down and #8 EZM12 as the thread to stitch, **Couch** (page 45) the stem and around the leaves.
► Using #8 EZM12, stitch a **Running Stitch** (page 26) in the center of each stripe on the fabric.
► Using a #3 Milliners needle and #8 EZM19, stitch **Bullion Knots** (page 92) around the base of the Lagoon wool layers of the leaves.

Three Small Leaves:

► Using #8 EZM12, stitch a **Chain Stitch** (page 169) around each leaf.
► Using #8 EZM12, stitch a **Closed Fly Stitch** (page 58) down the center of each leaf.
► Using a #3 Milliners needle and #8 EZM19, stitch **French Knots** (page 104) with two wraps at the end of each V of the Closed Fly Stitch.

Oceanfront Flower:

► Draw chalk lines for all the Couched lines from the center of the flower to the two Oriental Poppy velvet circles and from the base of the flower to the Mango ovals. Using #3 EZ30 with a #18 Chenille needle as the thread to lay down and #8 EZM19 as the thread to stitch, **Couch** (page 45) on all the chalk lines and around the Mango ovals.
► Using #8 EZM19, stitch a **Backstitch** (page 34) around the flower and the blue cotton layer.
► Using #8 EZM19, weave a **Pekinese Stitch** (page 40) through the backstitch on the top of the flower.
► Using a #3 Milliners needle and #8 EZM19, stitch **French Knots** (page 104) with two wraps on the base of the flower.

Vase:

► Using a #18 Chenille needle and #3 EZM101 as the backstitch and #8 EZM04 as the weaving thread, stitch a **Whipped Backstitch** (page 35) around the vase.
► Using RZM19, stitch half filled **Trellis Stitches** (page 114) about five rounds on five of the circles.
► Using DZ1113, stitch a **Backstitch** (page 34) around the other four circles.

Block 2
Finished Size: 10" x 15" + ¼ " Seam Allowance

Appliqué Threads:

Ellana Wool Thread:
EN08 Turquoise
EN09 Amazon Green
EN10 Spring Leaf
EN13 Electric Lime
EN18 Lagoon
EN23 Flamingo
EN59 Dogwood Rose

Efina Cotton Thread:
EF19 Sea Spray
EF35 Old Gold
EF43 Dark Cerise

Embellishment Threads:

Eleganza Perle Cotton:
#8 EZ04 Manatee
#8 EZM12 Inchworm
#8 EZM19 Island Oasis
#8 EZM36 Plush Lilac
#8 EZM81 Victory Bell
#8 EZM95 Battlefield
#8 EZM99 Treasure your Chest
#5 EZM100 Pinking up the Pieces
#3 EZ30 After Dinner Mint
#3 EZM07 Bee Pollen

Additional Threads:
Razzle RZM19 Pink Warrior

Background Fabrics:

Hand Dyed Wool:
Solid Black Wool

Cottons & More:
Black Dash
Smoke Silk
Black Alphabet Ribbon

Appliqué:

Hand Dyed Wool:
Amazon Green
Dogwood Rose
Electric Lime
Flamingo
Lagoon
Spring Leaf
Turquoise

Cottons & More:
Turquoise Square on Yellow
Yellow Dot on Mustard
Rainbow Swirl
Green Oriental Trees
Painter's Thread Ribbon Floss Cotton Tape Klimt
Beetroot Hand Dyed Velvet
Presto Sheer

Background Assembly:

Background:

Cut: Solid Black Wool - 10-½" x 15-½"

Background Layering:

For the layering, trace on freezer paper a 4-½" circle from the template provided on page 18. Cut it out on the pencil line and iron it to the back of the Black Dash fabric. Cut the fabric out a ¼" larger. With a contrasting color cotton thread, stitch a small **Running Stitch** (page 26) in the center of the seam allowance and draw it up so it molds around the freezer paper.

Cut: Smoke dupioni Silk - 2-½" x 6-½"

Pin the circle, Silk dupioni and calligraphy ribbon to the background, reference the photo on page 13 for placement. Appliqué in place removing the freezer paper and running stitch with tweezers from the circle just before finishing your appliqué. **Caution:** As this is a printed ribbon please do not iron it.

Appliqué:

Base of Leaves, Flowers and Vase:

Trace separately with a pencil on the matte side of your freezer paper the base elements for the flowers, leaves and vase. Cut out each of the freezer paper templates on the pencil line. Referring to the photograph, iron the templates to the appropriate color wool and cotton fabrics.

Center Stem:

Make a knot in the end of your Klimt Ribbon Floss Cotton, and thread into a #18 Chenille needle, bring your needle up from the back of your work, slightly left of center, at the top of your vase, and an ⅛" under the vase. Pull the thread all the way through to the front of your work so that the knot anchors the thread in the back, remove your needle. As this is a self ruching thread, simply pull one of the threads from the loose end of the ribbon and draw it up so that the tape ruches until it measures 4-¼" long. Vertically lay the ruched tape on your background to form the main stem. Manipulate the ruching so that the stem is even throughout and pin in place. Using a #3 Milliners needle and #8 EZM95 attach the tape to the background using three wrap **French Knots** (page 104). Cut out four ¾" Dogwood Rose wool circles, you can either use freezer paper templates or our ¾" wool punch. Referring to the photograph, appliqué all base pieces in place.

Layering of Leaves, Flowers and Vase:

For the layering of the leaves, flowers and vase cut templates out of freezer paper. Referring to the photograph, iron the templates to the appropriate color wool and cotton fabrics. Using a ½" wool punch, create five ½" circles for the flower from the Flamingo wool. Pin and appliqué the layering to the leaves, flowers and vase.

Hexagon Yo-Yo:

I love this dimensional technique taught to me by Dr. Peggy Rhodes and Julia Wood from their book 'Quick and Easy Hexie Quilts'.

Trace a 2" circle on your Presto Sheer stabilizer and cut out on the pencil line. Iron the Presto Sheer with the gritty side down (glue side) to the back of your Beetroot velvet. *Note: For the best results, use a warm iron and tap the Presto Sheer using the tip of the iron - long periods of direct heat will flatten the nap of the velvet.* Cut out the velvet around the edge of the presto sheer.

(1) With a pencil, mark the center of the circle on the Presto Sheer side. Thread a #3 Milliners needle with 12" of #8 EZM99 and knot the thread. (2) With the Presto Sheer side facing up, bring the needle up from the velvet side directly on the dot in the center of the circle until the knot catches on the velvet.

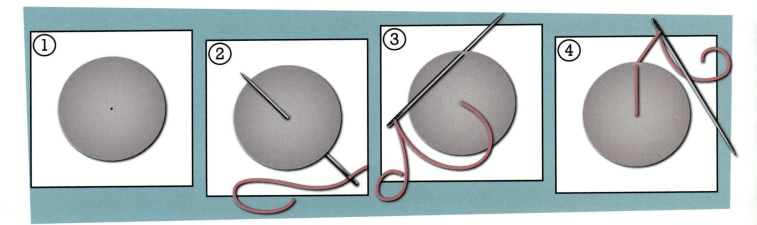

(3-5) With the Presto Sheer side facing up, insert your needle ⅛" in on the wrong side of the fabric at 12 o'clock, pulling the thread tight so that the edge of the circle meets the center of the circle.

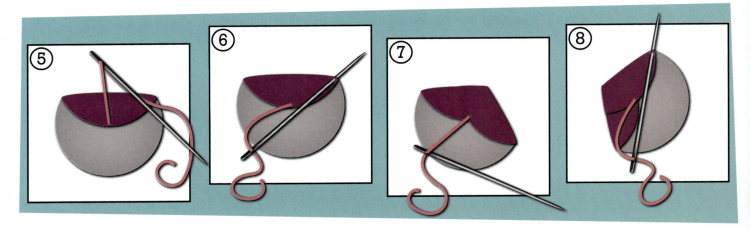

(6) Finger press the fold line. Insert your needle to the right about an ⅛" in where the two fabrics meet, making sure you go through both layers of fabric. (7-9) Pull the thread tight so that the right hand point folds to the center. Finger press the fold line and repeat working in a clockwise direction.

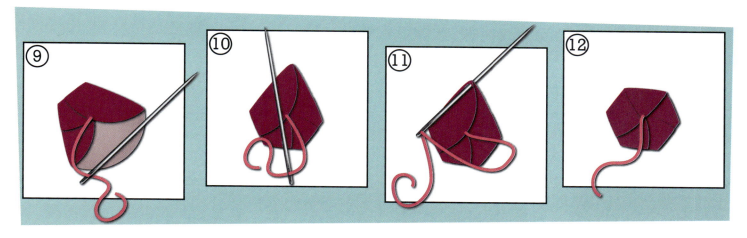

(10-12) For the last point, insert your needle through all three layers and pull your thread tight to form a hexagon. Knot the thread on the back, then sew the completed hexagon flower to your background using a cotton appliqué thread and the photograph for placement.

17

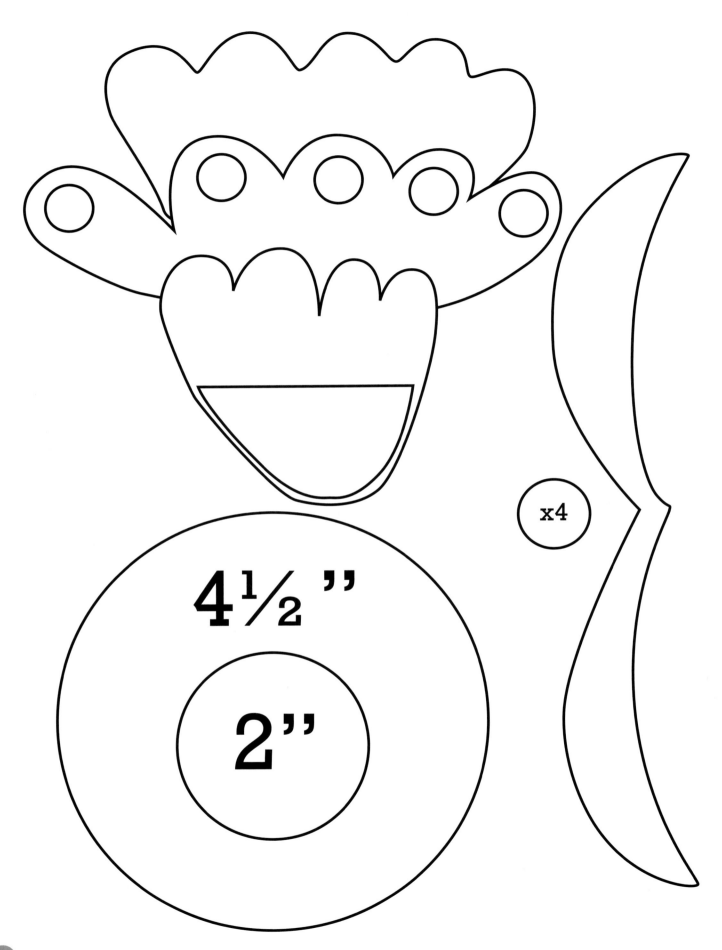

Embellish:

Background:

▶ Using a #3 Milliners needle and #8 EZ04, stitch **French Knots** (page 104) randomly in the Smoke dupioni Silk rectangle.

Spring Leaf Flower:

▶ Draw chalk lines connecting the large flower to the four Dogwood Rose wool circles.
▶ Using #8 EZM81 stitch a **Palestrina Knot** (page 68) on the chalk lines to connect the circles to the center flower.

Stems:

▶ Draw chalk lines from the stem to the Flamingo flowers and the Beetroot velvet hexagon yo-yo. Using a #18 Chenille needle with #3 EZM07 as the thread to lay down and a #3 Milliners needle with #8 EZM95 as the stitching thread, **Couch Using Bullion Knots** (page 47) using six wraps.

Large Center Flower:

▶ With a chalk pencil, draw the lines to divide the top of the Spring Leaf wool flower into four petals. Using a #18 Chenille needle and #3 EZ30 as the thread to lay down and #8 EZM12 as the stitching thread, **Couch** (page 45) around the flower's center and on the chalk lines to form four petals. Couch a smaller petal on the inside of each of the four petals.
▶ Using #8 EZM12, stitch a **Backstitch** (page 34) on the bottom edge of the cotton overlay.
▶ Using a #3 Milliners needle and #8 EZM19, stitch a row of **Cast On Bullion Knots** (page 164)

on the top edge of the cotton overlay using 30 cast ons.

▶ Using a #3 Milliners needle and #8 EZM99, stitch two rows of **Bullion Knots** (page 92) with each Bullion Knot connecting the base of the cast on with the adjacent cast on.

Electric Lime Leaves:

▶ Using #8 EZM12, stitch a small **Crested Chain Stitch** (page 124) around the edge of the leaves.
▶ Using #8 EZM12, stitch **Detached Chain Stitches** (page 52) on the leaves to add texture.

Dogwood Rose Circles:

▶ Using #8 EZM36 stitch a **Fly Stitch** (page 127) around the outer edge of each circle.
▶ Using a #3 Milliners needle and #8 EZM36, stitch a ring of **French Knots** (page 104) on each of the Dogwood Rose circles.

Gold Dot fabric:

▶ Using #8 EZM81, stitch a small **Italian Knotted Border Stitch** (page 62) around the outer edge of the gold dot fabric. *Tip: In each valley of the flower I stitched a couple of **Backstitches** (page 34) in order to avoid overlaying the stitches.*
▶ Using #8 EZM81, stitch a **Running Stitch** (page 26) around each of the printed circles on the fabric.

Turquoise Wool Flower:

▶ Using #8 EZM19, stitch a **Chain Stitch** (page 169) around the outer edge of the Turquoise section of the flower.
▶ Using #8 EZM19, stitch a **Seed Stitch** (page 55) on the bottom ⅔ of the Turquoise section of the flower.
▶ Using a #18 Chenille needle and #5 EZM100, stitch a **Backstitch** (page 34) around the five Flamingo circles.
▶ Using a #3 Milliners needle and #8 EZM99, stitch a **Bullion Rose** (page 110) in the center of each Flamingo circle.

Three Large Leaves:

▶ Using #8 EZM95, stitch a **Chain Stitch** (page 169) around each of the large leaves and around the outside edge of the wool veins on all three leaves.
▶ Using a #3 Milliners needle and #8 EZM81, stitch **French Knots** (page 104) ¼" apart using two wraps down the center of the leaf veins.

Vase:

▶ Using a #3 Milliners and #8 EZM95, stitch **Bullion Knots** (page 92) around the vase.
▶ Using #8 EZM95, stitch a **Chain Stitch** (page 169) around each of the rectangles on the vase.
▶ Using a #3 Milliners needle and #8 EZM95, stitch three **French Knots** (page 104) in each rectangle using two wraps.

Flamingo Flowers:

▶ With your chalk pencil draw three lines to form four separate petals at the base of both flowers. Using RZM19, stitch a **Backstitch** (page 34) on the chalk lines around the flowers and top edge of the cotton overlay.
▶ Using #3 Milliners needle and #8 EZM95, stitch a row of **Bullion Knots** (page 92) along the bottom edge of the cotton overlay.
▶ With your chalk pencil draw three stamens on each flower. Using a #18 Chenille needle and #3 EZ30 as the thread to lay down and #8 EZM12 as the stitching thread, **Couch** (page 45) the stamens in place.
▶ Using a #3 Milliners needle and #8 EZM12, stitch one **Double Cast On Stitch** (page 96) at the end of each stamen.
▶ Using a #3 Milliners needle and #8 EZM95, stitch a **Bullion Knot** (page 92) at the top of each cast on stitch.

Velvet Hexagon Yo-Yo:

▶ Using a #3 Milliners needle and #8 EZM19, stitch a cluster of **Drizzle Stitches** (page 100) using 25 cast ons in the center of the hexagon.

Block 3
Finished Size: 12" x 13" + ¼" Seam Allowance

Appliqué Threads:

Ellana Wool Thread:
EN08 Turquoise
EN11 Artichoke Heart
EN20 Cloud
EN21 Rhubarb
EN36 Orchid
EN47 Pumpkin
EN49 Kumquat
EN58 Lavender

Efina Cotton Thread:
EF02 Latte
EF08 Turquoise
EF11 Artichoke Heart
EF17 Blue Spruce
EF20 Cloud

Embellishment Threads:

Eleganza Perle Cotton:

#8 EZ51 Purple Sortie Cap
#8 EZM04 Carbon
#8 EZM12 Inchworm
#8 EZM19 Island Oasis
#8 EZM36 Plush Lilac
#8 EZM81 Victory Bell
#8 EZM95 Battlefield
#8 EZM99 Treasure your Chest
#5 EZM31 Hibiscus
#5 EZM100 Picking up the Pieces
#3 EZ30 After Dinner Mint

Additional Threads:
Razzle RZM3130 Aqua Sea
Painter's Thread #3 Perle Cotton Grandma Moses

Background Fabrics:

Hand Dyed Wool:
Black Solid Wool
Black Check Wool

Cottons & More:
Black Australian Words
Large White Dot on Black
Black Gold Metallic

Appliqué:

Hand Dyed Wool:
Artichoke Heart
Cloud
Kumquat
Lavender
Orchid
Pumpkin
Rhubarb
Turquoise

Cottons & More:
White Dot on Blue
Cream Line
Cloud Roman Glass
Green Triangles
Artichoke Heart Texture
Blue Spruce Silk
Cherry Hand Dyed Velvet
¾" Green Fanciful Stripes Ribbon

Background:

Cut: Black Solid Wool - 12-½" x 3-½" (A)
Black Check Wool - 12-½" x 2-½" (B) and 12-½" x 8-½" (C)

Sew B to A to C using a ¼" seam allowance and press the seams open.

Background Layering:

Cut: Black Australian Words Cotton - 2-¾" x 6"
Large White Dot on Black Cotton - 6-½" x 3-¾"
Black Gold Metallic Fabric - 2" x 2" (Cut Three)

Appliqué the layering pieces to the background using the photograph provided.

Appliqué:

Stems:

Cut: Striped ribbon main stem - cut 4-½"

Cut two bias strips from the Artichoke Heart Texture measuring ¾" x 3" and ¾" x 6". Pin and appliqué in place the two bias stems and the striped ribbon stem.

Base of Leaves, Flowers, Berries and Vase:

Trace separately with a pencil on the matte side of your freezer paper the base elements for the leaves, flowers, berries and vase. Cut out each of the freezer paper templates on the pencil line. Referring to the photograph, iron the templates to the appropriate color wool and cotton fabrics. Using your small appliqué pins, pin and appliqué all base layers in place.

Bird:

Appliqué, in place, the bird and beak, remembering to tuck a ¼" of the beak under the bird.

Layering of Leaves, Flowers, Vase and Bird:

For the layering of the flowers, leaves, vase and bird, cut templates out of freezer paper. Referring to the photograph, iron the templates to the appropriate color wool and cotton fabrics. For the Blue Spruce Silk, add a ¼" seam allowance so this can be needle turned in place. Using a ½" wool punch, create three ½" Kumquat circles for the left hand flower. Using a ¼" wool punch, create twelve ¼" Lavender circles for the right hand flower. Using a ⅜" punch, create five ⅜" Cloud circles for the main flower. Pin and appliqué the layering to the flowers, leaves and vase.

Velvet circles:

For the five Cherry velvet circles, trace five ¾" circles on your freezer paper, cut them out on the line, and iron to the wrong side of the velvet. I use a circle template to do these. Cut out the velvet adding a ¼" seam allowance. In the seam allowance, stitch a small basting stitch in a contrasting color cotton thread around each circle. Draw the basting thread up so that the seam allowance pulls up around the freezer paper. Appliqué the five velvet circles in place. Stitch ¾ of the way around each of these, remove the basting thread and freezer paper with tweezers then complete the stitching.

Embellish:

Background:

▶ Using #8 EZM04, stitch a **Running Stitch** (page 26) on the inside edge of each printed white circle.

Stems:

▶ Using #8 EZM12, stitch a **Closed Fly Stitch** (page 58) on the two bias cotton stems.

▶ Using #8 EZM81, stitch a **Running Stitch** (page 26) horizontally through each stripe of the ribbon.

▶ Using the diagram provided, draw chalk lines connecting the berries to the center stem and vase.

▶ Using #18 Chenille and Grandma Moses #3 Painters Thread, stitch a **Palestrina Knot** (page 68) from the berries to approximately 1-½" from the central stem. End by **Couching** (page 45) the Grandma Moses #3 Painters Thread with #8 EZM19. For the stem connecting to the vase, stitch only a **Palestrina Knot** (page 68).

Three small leaves:

▶ Using #3 Milliners needle and #8 EZM81, stitch **Cast on Bullion Knots** (page 164) on the top side of the leaves.

▶ Using #8 EZM81, stitch a **Chain Stitch** (page 169) along the bottom of the leaves.

▶ Using #3 Milliners needle and #8 EZM95, stitch **French Knots** (page 104) a ¼" apart around the edge of the Blue Spruce Silk inner leaves.

Two large leaves:

▶ Using a #18 Chenille needle and #3 EZ30 as the thread to lay down and #8 EZM95 as the stitching thread, **Couch** (page 45) using Cross Stitches around the bottom edge of the Artichoke Heart wool.

► Using #3 Milliners needle and #8 EZM81, stitch **Seed Stitches** (page 55), **French Knots** (page 104) and **Cross Stitches** throughout the Artichoke Heart wool section of the leaves.

Berries:

► Using #8 EZM19, stitch a **Chain Stitch** (page 169) around the outer edge of each Turquoise berry.
► Using #1 Milliners needle and #5 EZM100, stitch three **French Knots** (page 104) using two wraps on each berry.

Small Rhubarb Flower:

► For the stamens, draw chalk lines from the flower to the three Kumquat circles. Using Grandma Moses #3 Painters thread with a #18 Chenille needle as the thread to lay down and #8 EZM12 as the thread to stitch, **Couch** (page 45) over three chalk lines.
► Using #8 EZM99, stitch **Fly Stitches** (Page 127) around each Kumquat circle.
► Using #3 Milliners needle and #8 EZM99, stitch **French Knots** (page 104) randomly on each Kumquat circle.
► Using #18 Chenille needle and #5 EZM31, stitch a **Backstitch** (page 34) around the Rhubarb flower and top edge of the cotton fabric overlay.
► Draw five chalk lines from the base of the flower to the cotton overlay. Using #5 EZM31, stitch a **Backstitch** (page 34) over the chalk lines.
► Using a #3 Milliners needle and #8 EZM36, stitch **French Knots** (page 104) randomly at the base of the cotton overlay.
► Using #8 EZM12, stitch a **Running Stitch** (page 26) through the center of the green accent of the flower.

Cream Flower:

► Using #8 EZM19, stitch an **Italian Knotted Border Stitch** (page 62) around the outer edge of the cream cotton.
► Using #8 EZM95 as the thread you lay down and the stitching thread, **Couch** (page 45) lines connecting the ¼" Lavender circles to the Rhubarb center.
► Using #8 EZM36, stitch around the outer edge of the ¼" Lavender circles, alternating between a **Backstitch** (page 34) and a **Fly Stitch** (page 127).
► Using #3 Milliners needle and #8 EZM99, stitch a **Cast On Bullion Knot** (page 164) around the Rhubarb center.
► Using #8 EZM12, stitch a **Running Stitch** (page 26) at the top and bottom of the green accent of the flower.

Vase:

► Using #8 EZ51, stitch a **Chain Stitch** (page 169) around the outer edge of the vase and horizontally ¼" above the base.
► Using #8 EZ51, stitch a **Backstitch** (page 34) around each X.
► Using #3 Milliners needle and #8 EZ51, stitch two **Bullion Knots** (page 92) to form an X on each X. The base (horizontal) Bullion Knot has 12 wraps and the overlapping Bullion Knot (vertical) has 14 wraps.

Large Flower:

► Using a #18 Chenille needle and #5 EZM100, stitch a **Threaded Backstitch** (page 37) on the back edge of the flower.
► Using a #18 Chenille needle and #5 EZM31, stitch a **Threaded Backstitch** (page 37) on the top edge of the flower.
► Using a #18 Chenille needle and #5 EZM31, stitch a **Backstitch** (page 34) around the outer edge of the Kumquat flower.
► For the stamens, draw chalk lines from the flower to the five Cherry velvet circles. Using Grandma Moses #3 Painters thread with a #18 Chenille needle as the thread to lay down and #8 EZM12 as the thread to stitch, **Couch** (page 45) over the five chalk lines.
► Using a #3 Milliners needle and #8 EZ51, stitch **French Knots** (page 104) randomly in the center of the cotton overlay.
► Using Razzle 3130, stitch a **Backstitch** (page 34) around the five ⅜" Cloud circles.
► Using #8 EZM36, stitch a **Chain Stitch** (page 169) around the Lavender zigzag.

Bird:

► Using #18 Chenille needle and #5 EZM31, stitch a **Backstitch** (page 34) around the bird's beak.
► Using Razzle 3130, stitch a **Closed Fly Stitch** (page 58) around the birds body and a **Backstitch** (page 34) around the legs, tail and across the beak.
► Using Razzle 3130, stitch a **Closed Fly Stitch** (page 58) through each tail feather.
► Using #1 Milliners needle and #5 EZM31, stitch one wrap **French Knots** (page 104) at the end of each point of the Closed Fly Stitch on the tail feathers.

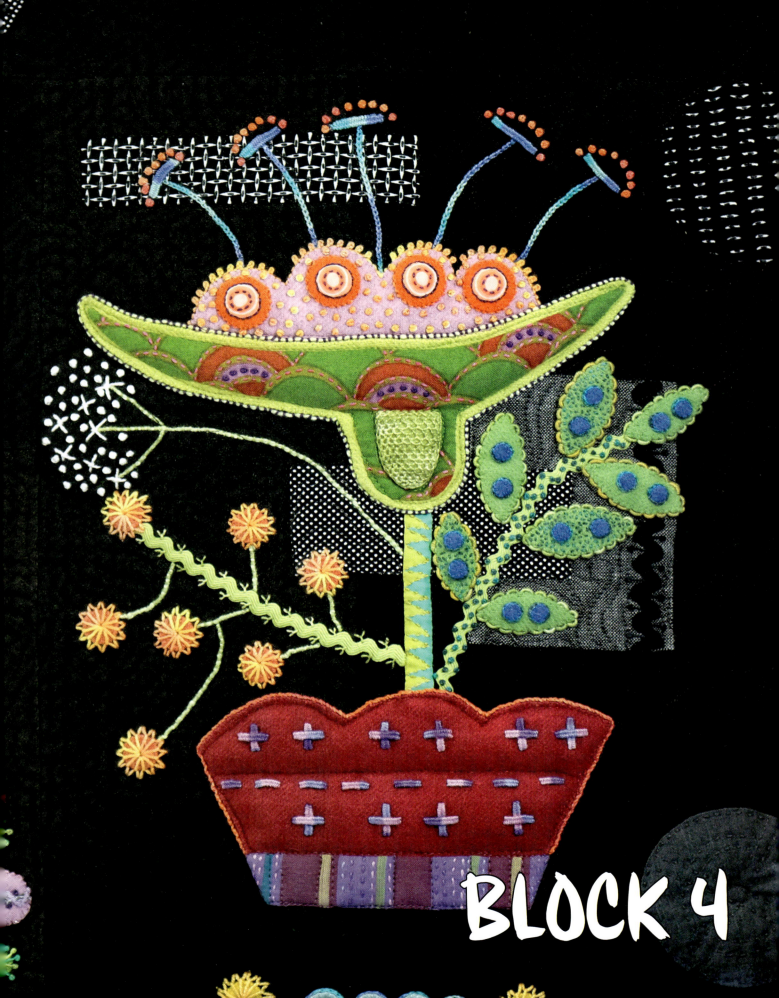

Block 4
Finished Size: 10" x 13" + ¼" Seam Allowance

Appliqué Threads:

Ellana Wool Thread:
EN10 Spring Leaf
EN14 Peridot
EN43 Dark Cerise
EN47 Pumpkin
EN48 Persimmon
EN56 Crystal Blue
EN59 Dogwood Rose

Efina Cotton Thread:
EF06 Charcoal
EF10 Spring Leaf
EF16 Pine Needle
EF30 Black
EF49 Kumquat
EF58 Lavender

Embellishment Threads:

Eleganza Perle Cotton:
#8 EZ51 Sortie Cap
#8 EZM04 Carbon
#8 EZM12 Inchworm
#8 EZM19 Island Oasis
#8 EZM36 Plush Lilac
#8 EZM81 Victory Bell
#8 EZM95 Battlefield
#8 EZM99 Treasure your Chest
#5 EZ06 Snow Globe
#5 EZM31 Hibiscus
#3 EZ30 After Dinner Mint

Other Threads:
The Thread Gatherer Silken Pearl Tuscan Sun

Background Fabrics:

Hand Dyed Wool:
Solid Black Wool
Plaid Black Wool

Cottons & More:
Black Essex
Black Mini Polka Dot
White Sphere on Black
½" wide Black Rick-Rack

Appliqué:

Hand Dyed Wool:
Crystal Blue
Dark Cerise
Dogwood Rose
Peridot
Persimmon
Pumpkin
Spring Leaf

Cottons & More:
Green Scallop
Purple Stripe
Orange Dot
⅜" wide Mint and Mustard Stems Ribbon
5/16" wide Spring Leaf Rick Rack

Background Assembly:

Background:

Cut: Solid Black wool - 6" x 13-½" (A)
Plaid Black wool - 5" x 13-½" (B)

Sew B to A using a ¼" seam allowance and press the seams open.

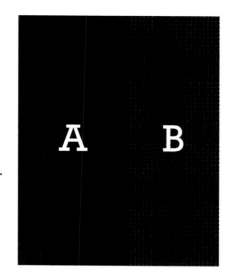

Background Layering:

Cut: Black Essex Cotton - 3-½" x 4-½"
Black Mini Polka Dot Cotton - 4-½" x 2"
White Sphere on Black Cotton - 5-½" x 1-½"
½" wide Black Rick Rack - 4-½"

Appliqué the layering pieces to the background using the photograph for placement. Appliqué the black rick rack an ⅛" in from the right hand side of the Black Essex layering piece.

Appliqué:

Stems:

Cut: ⅜" wide Mint and Mustard Stems - 3-¼"
⁵⁄₁₆" wide Spring Leaf rick rack - 4-¾" and 5-¼"

Pin and appliqué in place the two rick rack stems and the Mint and Mustard Stems ribbon.

Base of Leaves, Flower, Berries and Vase:

Trace separately with a pencil on the matte side of your freezer paper the base elements for the leaves, flower, berries and vase. Cut out each of the freezer paper templates on the pencil line. Using a ½" wool punch, create seven ½" Persimmon circles for the berries. Referring to the photograph, iron the templates to the appropriate color wool and cut out appliqué pieces. Using your small appliqué pins, pin and appliqué all base layers in place.

Layering of Leaves, Flower and Vase:

For the layering of the leaves, flower and vase cut templates out of freezer paper. Referring to the photograph, iron the templates to the appropriate color wool and cotton fabrics. Using a ¾" wool punch, create four ¾" Pumpkin circles for the center flower. Using a ¼" wool punch, create fourteen ¼" Crystal Blue circles for the leaves. Appliqué the layering to the leaves, flower and vase. **Note:** *When cutting your ½" cotton dots to layer on the Pumpkin circles, center each freezer template circle on a dot of the cotton fabric. Use the same technique used in blocks one and three for velvet circles to appliqué down the cotton dots.*

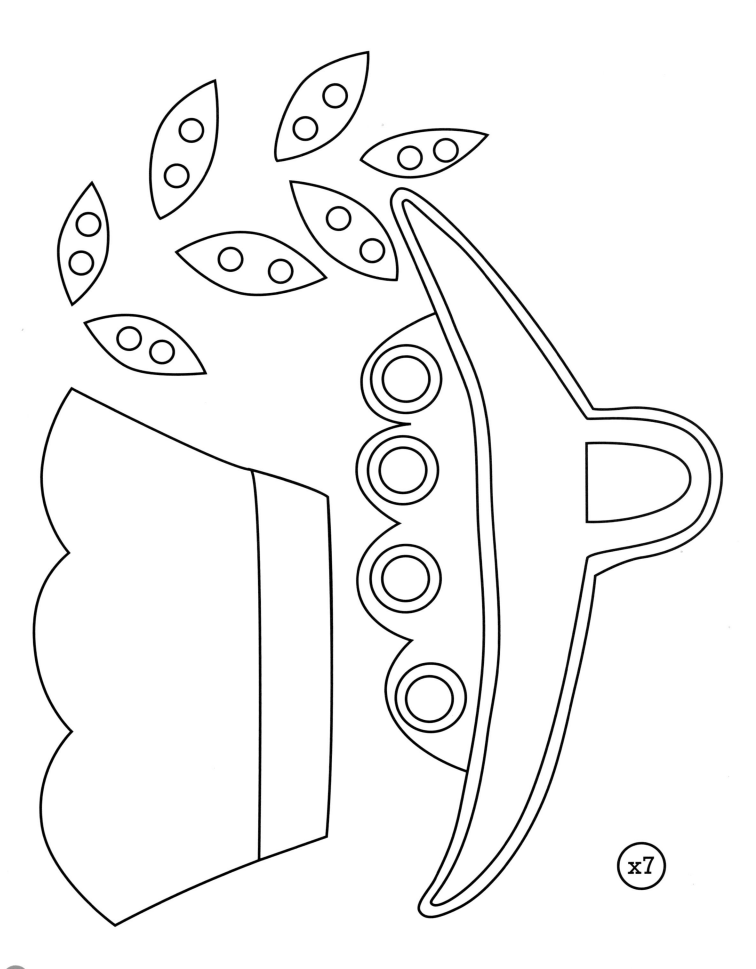

Embellish:

Background:

▶ Using a #3 Milliners needle and #8 EZM04, stitch a **Pistil Stitch** (page 106) with three wraps in each valley of the black rick rack.

Stems:

▶ Using #8 EZM81, stitch a **Running Stitch** (page 26) on the main stem following the zig zag of the Mint and Mustard Stems ribbon.
▶ Using #8 EZM12, stitch a small **Fly Stitch** (page 127) on the berry stem in the middle of each hill of the 5/16" wide Spring Leaf Rick Rack to form a thorny stem.
▶ Using a #3 Milliners needle and #8 EZM95 stitch two wrap **French Knots** (page 104) on the stem with leaves throughout the rick rack.
▶ Using the diagram provided draw chalk lines connecting the berries to the 5/16" wide Spring Leaf Rick Rack, the Baby Breath to the center stem and the flower stamens to the center flower. Using a #18 Chenille needle with #3 EZ30 as the thread to lay down and #8 EZM12 as the couching thread, **Couch** (page 45) over the chalk lines connecting the berries to the rick rack and the Baby Breath to the main stem.
▶ Using #8 EZM19, stitch a **Chain Stitch** (page 169) over the chalk lines connecting the stamens to the main flower.

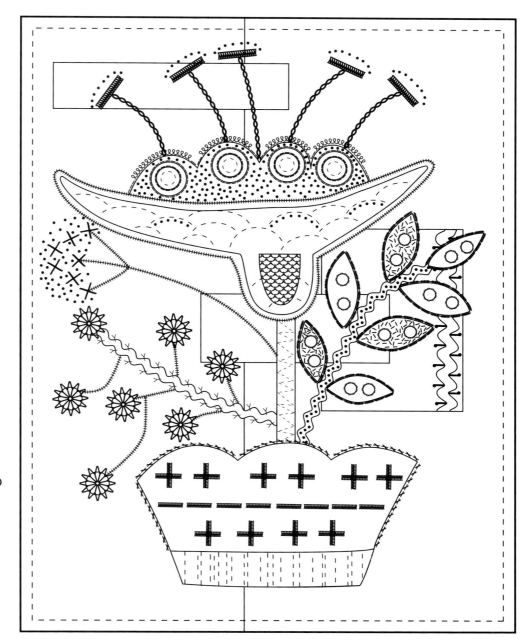

Leaves:

▶ Using a #3 Milliners needle and #8 EZM81, stitch **Bullion Knots** (page 92) around three of the Peridot leaves.
▶ Using a #3 Milliners needle and #8 EZM12, stitch **Bullion Knots** (page 92) around the remaining four Peridot leaves.
▶ Using #8 EZM95, stitch a **Chain Stitch** (page 169) around the ¼" Crystal Blue circles.
▶ Referring to the diagram, use #8 EZM95 to stitch a **Seed Stitch** (page 55) in three leaves.

Berries:

▶ Using Tuscan Sun Silken Pearl, stitch **Fly Stitches** (page 127) around each ¾" Persimmon circle connecting the base of each fly stitch to the center of the circle.

Baby Breath:

▶ Referring to the diagram, use a #18 Chenille needle and #5 EZ06 to stitch seven **Cross Stitches** at the top of the stem.
▶ Using a #1 Milliners needle and #5 EZ06, fill in to form the Baby Breath with three wrap **French Knots** (page 104).

Flower:

▶ Using a #18 Chenille needle and #5 EZM31, stitch a **Backstitch** (page 34) around the ¾" Pumpkin circles.
▶ Using #8 EZ51, stitch a **Backstitch** (page 34) around the outer edge of the orange dot cotton fabric.
▶ Using #8 EZ51, stitch a **Running Stitch** (page 26) to form a circle in the center of each orange dot.
▶ Using a #18 Chenille needle and Tuscan Sun Silken Pearl, stitch a **Rosette Chain** (page 129) around the top edge of the Dogwood Rose wool. ***Note:*** *I stitched three **Backstitches** (page 34) to start the Rosette Chain and in and out of each valley.*
▶ Using a #1 Milliners needle and Tuscan Sun Silken Pearl, stitch two wrap **French Knots** (page 104) throughout the Dogwood Rose wool.
▶ Using #3 EZ30 with a #18 Chenille needle as the thread to lay down and #8 EZ51 as the thread to stitch, **Couch** (page 45) around the Spring Leaf base of the flower.
▶ Following the design in the cotton fabric of the flower base, use #8 EZM99 to stitch **Running Stitches** (page 26) through the green semi circles.
▶ Using #8 EZ51, stitch three wrap **French Knots** (page 104) through three semi circles of your print.
▶ Using #8 EZM12, stitch an **Open Buttonhole Filler Stitch** (page 141) over the Spring Leaf overlay at the base of the flower. To weave, either use the back end of a #3 Milliners needle or a Tapestry needle (these have a blunt point).
▶ Using a #3 Milliners needle and #8 EZM19, stitch a ¾" horizontal two thread **Needle Weave Bar** (page 166) at the top of each Chain Stitch stamen.
▶ Using a #1 Milliners needle and #5 EZM31, stitch eight three wrap **French Knots** (page 104) forming a semi circle above each Needle Weave Bar.

Vase:

▶ Using a #18 Chenille needle and #5 EZM31, stitch a **Whipped Backstitch** (page 35) around the outer edge of the Dark Cerise wool of the vase.
▶ Using #8 EZM36, stitch vertical rows of **Running Stitches** (page 26) through the Lavender sections of the striped cotton fabric.
▶ Referring to the stitch diagram, use a #3 Milliners needle and #8 EZM36 to stitch ½" **Needle Weave Bars** (page 166) forming two rows of crosses and one row of dashes on the Dark Cerise vase.

Block 5
Finished Size: 12" x 13" + ¼" Seam Allowance

Appliqué Threads:

Ellana Wool Thread:
EN09 Amazon Green
EN13 Electric Lime
EN31 Creamed Butter
EN42 Holly Berry
EN47 Pumpkin

Efina Cotton Thread:
EF06 Charcoal
EF10 Spring Leaf
EF18 Lagoon
EF19 Sea Spray
EF20 Cloud
EF30 Black
EF34 Sun Yellow
EF36 Orchid

Embellishment Threads:
Eleganza Perle Cotton:

#8 EZ51 Sortie Cap
#8 EZM04 Carbon
#8 EZM14 Lettuce Wrap
#8 EZM19 Island Oasis
#8 EZM36 Plush Lilac
#8 EZM95 Battlefield

#8 EZM99 Treasure your Chest
#5 EZM31 Hibiscus
#5 EZM82 Haymaker's Punch
#3 EZM07 Bee Pollen
#3 EZM101 Fight Like a Girl

Other Threads:
Painter's Thread #3 Perle Cotton Grandma Moses
Dazzle DZ1113 Survivor
Razzle RZM3130 Aqua Sea
Razzle RZM19 Pink Warrior

Background Fabrics:

Hand Dyed Wool:
Plaid Black Wool
Solid Black Wool
Textured Black Wool

Cottons & More:
Black Silver Metallic Cotton
White Sphere on Black

Appliqué:

Hand Dyed Wool:
Holly Berry
Pumpkin
Creamed Butter
Amazon Green
Electric Lime

Cottons & More:
Purple Ferns
Yellow Ribbon Stripe
Turquoise Crosses on Green
Green with Pins
Aqua with Button Flowers
⅜" wide Aqua Green Stems
5/16" wide Lagoon Rick Rack

Background Assembly:

Background:

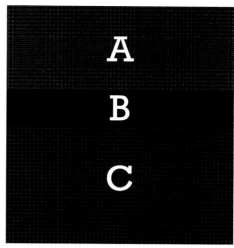

Cut: Plaid Black Wool - 5" x 12-½" (A)
Solid Black Wool - 2-½" x 12-½" (B)
Textured Black Wool - 7" x 12-½" (C)

Using ¼" seam allowance sew A to B, then to C, press the seams open.

Background Layering:

For the layering trace on freezer paper a 5-½" circle from the pattern provided. Cut it out on the pencil line and iron it to the back of the Black Silver Metallic fabric. Cut the fabric out a ¼" larger. With a contrasting color cotton thread stitch a small running stitch in the center of the seam allowance and draw it up so it molds around the freezer paper. For large circles I like to use the heavy duty freezer paper (available on our website) as its strong features keep a better shape for larger circles.

Cut: White Sphere on Black Cotton - 6" x 2-½"

Pin the circle and the White Sphere on Black to the background. Appliqué in place removing with tweezers the freezer paper and running stitch from the circle just before finishing your appliqué.

Appliqué:

Main Stem:

Cut the ⅜" wide Aqua Green Stems ribbon down to 2". Referring to the photograph pin and appliqué in place the Aqua Green Stems ribbon.

Base of Leaves, Flowers, Berries and Vase:

Trace separately with a pencil on the matte side of your freezer paper the base elements for the leaves, flowers, berries and vase. Cut out each of the freezer paper templates on the pencil line. Using a ¾" wool punch, create nine ¾" Creamed Butter circles for the center flower stamens. Referring to the photograph iron the templates to the appropriate color wool and cut out appliqué pieces. Using your small appliqué pins, pin then appliqué all base layers in place except the vase, as the Lagoon rick rack stems will need to be tucked under the vase.

Layering of Leaves, Flower and Vase:

For the layering of the leaves, flower and vase cut templates out of freezer paper. Referring to the photograph, iron the templates to the appropriate color wool and cotton fabrics. **Note:** *I centered five vertical stripes on the main flower layering fabric.* Appliqué the layering to the flower and cotton layer to the leaves. Appliqué the 5⁄16" wide Lagoon rick rack in place. Using a

⅜" and ½" wool punch, create four ⅜" and two ½" Amazon Green circles for the large leaves and appliqué in place. Appliqué the vase in place, tucking the Lagoon rick rack and main stem under the top edge of the vase. Finish by appliquéing the zig zag layering on the vase.

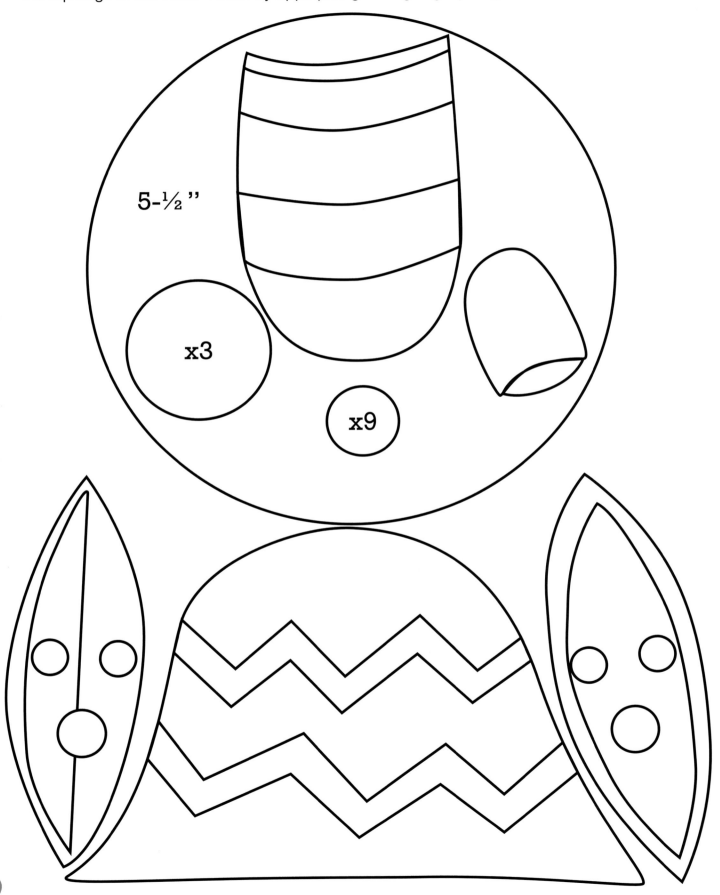

Embellish:

Background:

▶ Using #8 EZM04, stitch horizontal and vertical rows of small **Running Stitches** (page 26) through the center of the white of the White Sphere on Black.

Stems:

▶ Using the diagram provided, draw chalk lines connecting the large stamens to the main flower, the two cotton flowers to the sides of the main flower, the ⅜" Lagoon circles to the ⁵⁄₁₆" wide Lagoon rick rack, and the flowers on the left hand side to the vase.

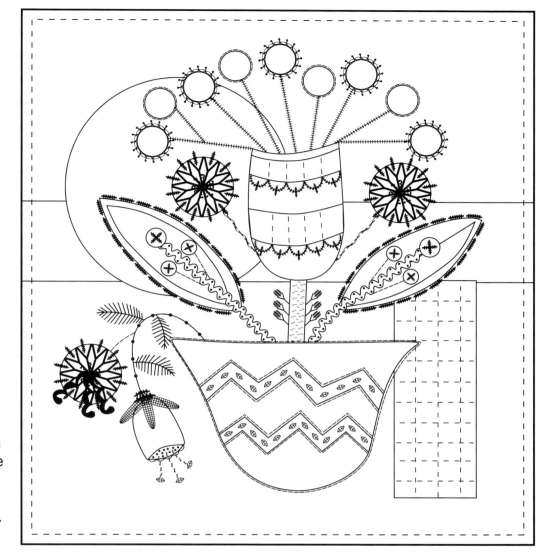

▶ Using #3 EZM07 with a #18 Chenille needle as the thread to lay down and #8 EZM36 as the couching thread, **Couch** (page 45) over the chalk lines connecting the Creamed Butter berries to the main flower.
▶ Using Grandma Moses #3 Painters Thread, stitch a **Threaded Backstitch** (page 37) on the chalk lines connecting the cotton flowers to the sides of the main flower.
▶ Using #3 EZM07, stitch a **Palestrina Knot** (page 68) from the vase to the purple Bell Flower and a **Backstitch** (page 34) from the Palestrina Knot stem to the cotton circle flower.
▶ Using Grandma Moses #3 Painters Thread, stitch a **Backstitch** (page 34) connecting the ⅜" Lagoon circles to the ⁵⁄₁₆" wide Lagoon rick rack stem.
▶ Using #8 EZM95, stitch two wrap **French Knots** (page 104) on the hills of the ⁵⁄₁₆" wide Lagoon Rick Rack stems.
▶ Using #8 EZM14, stitch a **Running Stitch** (page 26) on the main stem following the zig zag of the Aqua Green Stems ribbon.
▶ Using a #3 Milliners needle and #8 EZM95, stitch three small **Fly Stitches** (page 127) at 45 degrees on either side of the main stem and a **Bullion Knot** (page 92) in the center of each V.
▶ Using a #3 Milliners needle and #8 EZM14, stitch a **Bullion Knot** (page 92) on either side of the central Bullion Knot in the V of each Fly Stitch.

Leaves:

▶ Using a #3 Milliners needle and #8 EZM14, stitch **Bullion Knots** (page 92) around the outer edge of the two large leaves and two **Bullion Knots** (page 92) to form an X in each of the Lagoon circles.

▶ Using your chalk pencil draw three small leaves on the Palestrina Knot Stem. Using a #18 Chenille needle and Grandma Moses #3 Painters Thread, stitch a **Closed Fly Stitch** (page 58) following the shape of your drawn leaves and stitching the rows close together.

Main Flower:

▶ Referring to the diagram, use a #18 Chenille Needle and #5 EZM82 to stitch around the outer edge of five berries with a **Crested Chain Stitch** (page 124) and the outer edge of the other four berries with a **Backstitch** (page 34).

▶ Using a #1 Milliners needle and #5 EZM82, stitch five (twenty cast on) **Cast On Bullion Knots** (page 164) across the flower aligning each Cast On Bullion Knot with the stripe in the fabric on the bottom of both striped flower overlays.

▶ Referring to the diagram, use a #3 Milliners needle and #8 EZM19, attach each Cast On Bullion Knot by stitching a **Bullion Knot** (page 92) in the center of each Cast On Bullion Knot.

▶ Using #18 Chenille needle and #5 EZM82, stitch a vertical **Running Stitch** (page 26) on the printed vertical line of each stripe of the flower overlay.

Three Cotton Flowers:

▶ Using #8 EZM19, stitch **Fly Stitches** (page 127) around the cotton flowers, bringing the tail of each Fly Stitch to the center point of each circle.

▶ Using a #1 Milliners needle and #5 EZM31, stitch **Bullion Knots** (page 92) in each V of the Fly Stitches, extending each Bullion Knot into the background.

▶ Using a #3 Milliners needle and #8 EZM36, stitch three long, twenty five wrap **Drizzle Stitches** (page 100) in the center of the bottom left cotton circular flower.

▶ Using a #3 Milliners needle and #8 EZ51, stitch a cluster of ten wrap **Drizzle Stitches** (page 100) in the center of each cotton flower and around the three long Drizzle Stitches already stitched in #8 EZM36.

Purple Bell Flower:

▶ Using #8 EZM14, stitch three **Woven Picots** (page 148) at the top of the flower. Finish by adding two horizontal **Bullion Knots** (page 92) at the base of the stem in #8 EZM14.

▶ Using #8 EZM99, stitch a **Chain Stitch** (page 169) at the base of the Pumpkin wool.

▶ Using your chalk pencil draw three stamens from the center of the Pumpkin wool. Using #8 EZM14, stitch a **Whipped Backstitch** (page 35) on each chalk line.

▶ Using a #1 Milliners needle and DZ1113, stitch two wrap **French Knots** (page 104) on the Pumpkin wool.

▶ Using a #1 Milliners needle and RZ3130, stitch a **Double Cast On Stitch** (page 96) horizontally on the end of each stamen.

Vase:

▶ Using a #18 Chenille needle and #3 EZM101, stitch a **Backstitch** (page 34) around the outer edge of the Holly Berry wool of the vase and the Pumpkin overlay.

▶ Using a #1 Milliners needle and RZM19, stitch ¼" **Double Cast On Stitches** (page 96) with fourteen cast ons through the center of the Pumpkin zig zags.

BLOCK 6

Block 6
Finished Size: 10" x 15" + ¼" Seam Allowance

Appliqué Threads:

Ellana Wool Thread:
EN10 Spring Leaf
EN18 Lagoon
EN22 Raspberry
EN47 Pumpkin
EN49 Kumquat
EN53 Baby Blue
EN59 Dogwood Rose

Efina Cotton Thread:
EF06 Charcoal
EF08 Turquoise
EF10 Spring Leaf
EF30 Black

Embellishment Threads:

Eleganza Perle Cotton:
#8 EZ51 Sortie Cap
#8 EZM04 Carbon
#8 EZM19 Island Oasis
#8 EZM36 Plush Lilac
#8 EZM81 Victory Bell
#8 EZM95 Battlefield
#8 EZM99 Treasure your Chest
#5 EZM31 Hibiscus
#5 EZM82 Haymaker's Punch
#5 EZM93 Marsh Grass
#3 EZ30 After Dinner Mint
#3 EZM101 Fight Like a Girl

Other Threads:
Painter's Thread #3 Perle Cotton Grandma Moses
Dazzle DZ1113 Survivor
Razzle RZM3130 Aqua Sea
Razzle RZM19 Pink Warrior
The Thread Gatherer 4mm Silk Ribbon Pond Scum
The Thread Gatherer Silken Pearl Tuscan Sun

Background Fabrics:

Hand Dyed Wool:
Solid Black Wool
Striped Black Wool

Cottons & More:
Hill Dash on Black
Black Grunge
⅜" wide Black with White Dot Ribbon

Appliqué:

Hand Dyed Wool:
Pumpkin
Spring Leaf
Baby Blue
Raspberry
Lagoon
Dogwood Rose
Kumquat

Cottons & More:
Green Paperweights on Black
Blue Stripe
Artichoke Heart Crackle
⅝" wide Blue Flower Wheel on Green Ribbon

Background Assembly:

Background:

Cut: Solid Black Wool - 5-¼" x 15-½" (A)
Striped Black Wool - 5-¾" x 15-½" (B)

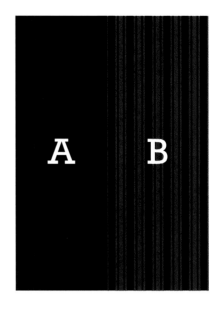

Sew A to B using a ¼" seam allowance and press the seams open.

Background Layering:

Cut: Black Hill Dash Cotton - 6" x 6"
Black Grunge Cotton - 5" x 2"
⅜" wide Black with White Dot Ribbon - 4-½"

Referring to the photograph, pin the two background pieces and ribbon in place. Appliqué all background layering in place.

Appliqué:

Main Stem:

Cut: Chartreuse Crackle Cotton - ¾" x 4-½".

Referring to the photograph pin and appliqué the stem in place.

Base of Leaves, Flowers, Berries and Vase:

Trace separately with a pencil on the matte side of your freezer paper the base elements for the leaves, flowers, berries and vase. Using a ¾" wool punch, create four ¾" Raspberry circles for the berries. Referring to the photograph, iron the templates to the appropriate color wool and cotton fabrics and cut out appliqué pieces. Using your small appliqué pins, pin and appliqué all base layers in place except the Baby Blue flower on the left-hand side of the block.

Layering of Leaves, Flower and Vase:

For the layering of the leaves and vase cut templates out of freezer paper. Referring to the photograph, iron the templates to the appropriate color wool and cotton fabrics. Using a ¾" wool punch, create four ¾" Kumquat circles for the vase. Appliqué the layering to the leaves and vase. Referring to the photograph, appliqué the Baby Blue flower to the left of the block overlapping the Pumpkin vase and the ⅝" wide Blue Flower Wheel on Green ribbon on the main flower.

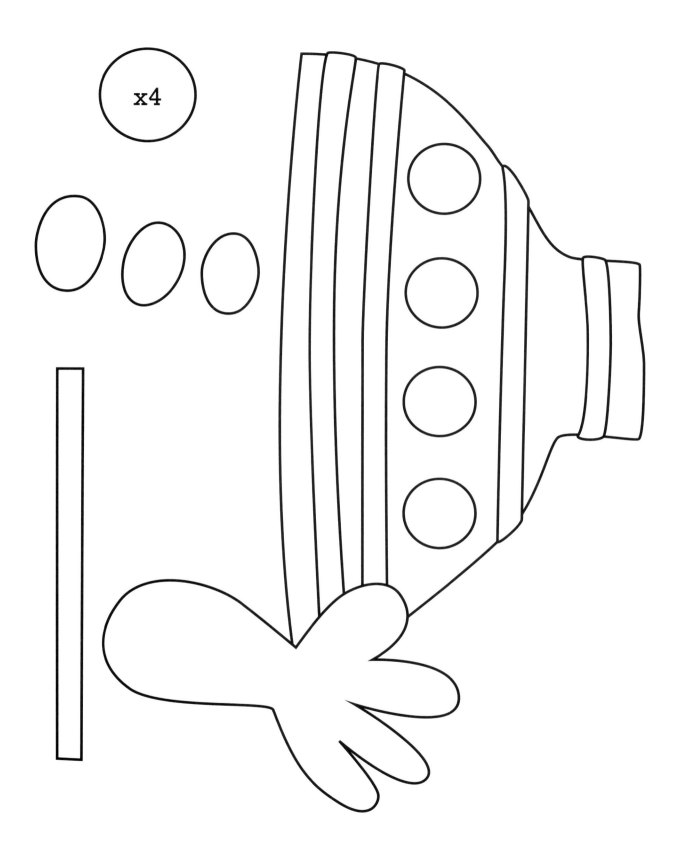

Embellish:

Background:

▶ Using #8 EZM04, stitch small **Running Stitches** (page 26) through the center of the white dash of the Black Hill Dash fabric.

Stems:

▶ Referring to the diagram provided, draw chalk lines connecting the Raspberry berries and Baby Blue flower to the main stem, three stamens to the Baby Blue flower, three Dogwood Rose berries to the vase, three stamens to the top of the main flower, and the two stems holding leaves.

▶ Using #5 EZM93 with a #18 Chenille needle as the thread to lay down and the couching thread, **Couch** (page 45) over the chalk lines connecting the Raspberry berries and Baby Blue flower to the main stem.

▶ Using Grandma Moses #3 Painters Thread with a #18 Chenille needle as the thread to lay down and #5 EZM93 as the couching thread, **Couch** (page 45) over the chalk lines for the stamens on the Baby Blue flower and the main flower.

▶ Using Grandma Moses #3 Painters Thread with a #18 Chenille needle as the thread to lay down and the couching thread, **Couch** (page 45) over the chalk lines connecting the Dogwood Rose berries to the vase.

▶ Using Grandma Moses #3 Painters Thread with a #18 Chenille needle as the thread to lay down and #8 EZM81 as the couching thread, **Couch Using Bullion Knots** (page 47) over the chalk lines for the two stems that will hold leaves.

Leaves:

► Using a #18 Chenille needle and #5 EZM93, stitch a **Backstitch** (page 34) around the cotton overlay of the Lagoon leaves.
► Using #8 EZM95, stitch **Closed Fly Stitch** (page 58) around the outer edge of the three Lagoon leaves.
► Using #8 EZM93, stitch **Running Stitches** (page 26) through the circles of the cotton overlay on the Lagoon leaves.
► Referring to the diagram for placement use a #3 Milliners Needle and 4mm Pond Scum Silk Ribbon to stitch twelve small **Closed Fly Stitch** (page 58) leaves on the two stems on the main flower. *Tip:* Cut your silk ribbon at an angle - this helps prevent fraying.

Working with Silk Ribbon:
Silk ribbon tends to slip out the eye of the needle when stitching, follow these steps to secure the ribbon:
- Thread the ribbon through the eye of the needle.
- Centered and about a ¼" from the end, pierce the end of the ribbon with the needle.
- Pull the long end of the ribbon down.
- Tighten the ribbon until it's securely locked in the needle's eye.

Main Flower:

► Referring to the diagram, use a #1 Milliners Needle and #5 EZM31 to stitch two **Bullion Knots** (page 92) to form a cross at the end of the three stamens.
► Using #8 EZM19, stitch a **Running Stitch** (page 26) in the center of each stripe of the woven fabric.
► Using a #1 Milliners needle and DZ1113, stitch twenty four wrap **Drizzle Stitches** (page 100) on the top edge of the Blue Flower Wheel ribbon starting at the right edge working to the left edge, leaving a ¼" between each drizzle stitch.
► Using a #1 Milliners needle and RZM19 and a #3 Milliners needle and #8 EZM99, stitch twenty four wrap **Drizzle Stitches** (page 100) to fill in the ¼" spaces on the top edge of the Blue Flower Wheel ribbon.
► Using a #18 Chenille needle for the backstitch and a Tapestry needle (or the back of a #15 Milliners needle) for the Buttonhole Filler Stitch with a #3 EZ30, stitch a **Double Open Buttonhole Filler Stitch** (page 141) over the Spring Leaf wool.
► Using #8 EZM95, stitch individual **Chain Stitches** (page 169) down the center of the main stem.
► Using a #3 Milliners needle as the anchor needle and a Tapestry needle (or the back of a #15 Milliners needle) for the weaving with #3 EZM101, stitch five **Woven Picots** (page 148) on the base of the main flower.

Berries:

► Using #8 EZM99, stitch a **Fly Stitch** (page 127) around the outer edge of the four Raspberry berries.
► Using #8 EZM36, stitch a **Chain Stitch** (page 169) around the outer edge of the three Dogwood Rose berries.
► Using a #3 Milliners needle and #8 EZM36, stitch three **Pistil Stitches** (page 106) at the base of each Dogwood Rose berry.

▶ Using #8 EZM36, stitch a **Closed Tete de Boeuf Stitch** (page 135) down the center of each Dogwood Rose berry.

Baby Blue Flower:

▶ Using RZ3130, stitch a **Chain Stitch** (page 169) around the outer edge of the Baby Blue flower.
▶ Referring to the diagram, use 4mm Pond Scum Silk Ribbon to stitch seven ½" **Detached Chain Stitches** (page 52) on the top edge of the Baby Blue flower to form a leafy sepal, followed by two horizontal **Backstitches** (page 34) on top of each other to connect the sepal to the stem.
▶ Using a #15 Milliners needle and #3 EZM101, stitch a **French Knot** (page 104) at the base of each of the Silk Ribbon Chain Stitches.
▶ Using RZ3130, stitch **Detached Chain Stitches** (page 52) on the upper part of the Baby Blue flower.
▶ Using a #15 Milliners needle and #3 EZM101, stitch a horizontal **Needle Weave Bar** (page 166) across the center of the Baby Blue flower.
▶ Using a #3 Milliners needle and #8 EZ51 and #8 EZM81, stitch a cluster of **Drizzle Stitches** (page 100) under the Needle Weave Bar.
▶ Referring to the diagram, using a #1 Milliners Needle and #5 EZM31, stitch two **Bullion Knots** (page 92) to form a cross at the end of the three stamens.
▶ Using #15 Milliners needle and #3 EZM101, stitch three **French Knots** (page 104) in a vertical row below the Bullion Knot cross stitches.

Vase:

▶ Using a #18 Chenille needle and Silken Pearl Tuscan Sun, stitch a **Backstitch** (page 34) around the outer edge of the Pumpkin vase.
▶ Using a #18 Chenille needle and #5 EZM31, stitch a **Backstitch** (page 34) around the outer edge of the four Kumquat circles.
▶ Using a #1 Milliners needle and #5 EZM82, stitch a vertical **Double Cast-on Stitch** (page 96) in the center of the four Kumquat circles.
▶ Using a #18 Chenille needle for the backstitch and a Tapestry needle (or the back of a #1 Milliners needle) for the weaving and #5 EZM82, stitch a **Threaded Double Backstitch** (Explanation found on page 116) on the first Kumquat stripe, with your Backstitches on either side of the Kumquat stripe.
▶ Using a #18 Chenille needle for the backstitch and either a Tapestry needle (or the back of a #1 Milliners needle) for the weaving and #5 EZM82, stitch a **Threaded Backstitch** (page 37) on the outer edges of the second and third Kumquat stripe.
▶ Using a #18 Chenille needle for the backstitch and either a Tapestry needle (or the back of a #1 Milliners needle) for the weaving and #5 EZM82, stitch a **Double Threaded Double Backstitch Variation** (Explanation found on page 116) on the fourth Kumquat stripe, with your Backstitches on either side of the Kumquat stripe.

Block 7
Finished Size: 10" x 15" + ¼ " Seam Allowance

Appliqué Threads:

Ellana Wool Thread:
EN14 Peridot
EN17 Blue Spruce
EN19 Sea Spray
EN22 Raspberry
EN34 Sun Yellow
EN47 Pumpkin
EN49 Kumquat
EN58 Lavender
EN60 Deep Teal

Efina Cotton Thread:
EF06 Charcoal
EF10 Spring Leaf
EF12 Avocado
EF19 Sea Spray
EF30 Black
EF47 Pumpkin

Embellishment Threads:

Eleganza Perle Cotton:

#8 EZM04 Carbon
#8 EZM12 Inchworm
#8 EZM14 Lettuce Wrap
#8 EZM19 Island Oasis
#8 EZM36 Plush Lilac
#8 EZM81 Victory Bell
#8 EZM95 Battlefield
#8 EZM99 Treasure your Chest
#5 EZ11 Heavy Skies
#5 EZM82 Haymaker's Punch
#3 EZM101 Fight Like a Girl

Other Threads:
Painter's Thread #3 Perle Cotton Grandma Moses
Painter's Thread Soft Cotton Rousseau
Razzle RZ3130 Aqua Sea
The Thread Gatherer Silken Pearl Tuscan Sun

Background Fabrics:

Hand Dyed Wool:
Black Textured Wool
Black Solid Wool

Cottons & More:
Black Floral Words
Black Small Polka Dot

Appliqué:

Hand Dyed Wool:
Blue Spruce
Deep Teal
Kumquat
Lavender
Peridot
Pumpkin
Raspberry
Sea Spray
Sun Yellow

Cottons & More:
Birds and Flowers on Orange
Sea Spray Grunge
Avocado Grunge
White Crosses on Avocado

Background Assembly:

Background:

Cut: Textured Black Wool - 6-½" x 10-½" (A)
Solid Black Wool - 9-½" x 10-½" (B)

Sew A to B using a ¼" seam allowance, press the seams open.

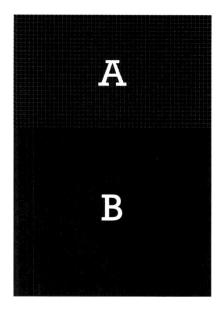

Background Layering:

Cut: Black Floral Words Cotton - 10-½" x 2-½"
Black Small Polka Dot Cotton - 4-½" x 4-½"
Black Small Polka Dot Cotton - 2-½" x 2-½"

Referring to the photograph, pin the three background pieces in place. Appliqué all background layering in place.

Appliqué:

Main Stem:

Cut Avocado Grunge fabric center stem - ¾" x 7". Referring to the photograph, pin and appliqué the stem in place.

Base of leaves, flowers, berries and vase:

Trace separately with a pencil on the matte side of your freezer paper the base elements for the leaves, flowers, berries and vase. Using a ½" wool punch, create three ½" Sun Yellow circles for the top of the flower. Using a ¾" wool punch, create three ¾" Raspberry circles for the berries. Referring to the photograph, iron the templates to the appropriate color wool and cotton fabrics and cut out appliqué pieces, remembering to add a ¼" to the bottom of the Sea Spray accent to tuck under the Pumpkin flower. Using your small appliqué pins, pin and appliqué all base layers in place. For the large flower appliqué the orange cotton fabric to the top of the stem. Position your Pumpkin flower in place, tuck under and sew in place the Sea Spray accent before sewing the Pumpkin flower in place.

Layering of large leaf and vase:

For the layering of the leaf cut out your freezer paper template and wool appliqué for the center Blue Spruce accent. Using a ½" wool punch, create four ½" Blue Spruce circles for the leaf. Using a ¾" wool punch, create nine ¾" Deep Teal circles for the vase. Appliqué the layering to the leaf and vase.

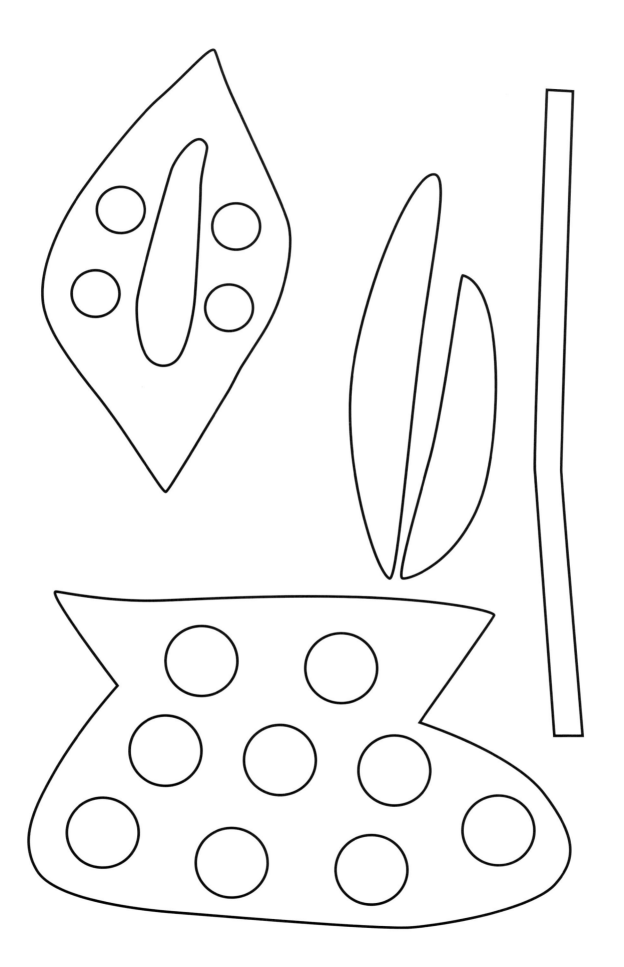

Embellish:

Background:

▶ Using #8 EZM04, stitch small **Fly Stitches** (page 127) along the top edge of the word fabric. In the center of each V of the Fly Stitch, stitch a ¼" **Bullion Knot** (page 92).

Stems:

▶ Using the diagram provided, draw chalk lines connecting the Sun Yellow berries to the top of the Pumpkin flower, the Kumquat ovals to the Sea Spray grunge flower, the Raspberry berries to the main stem and vase, and the small flower to the Raspberry berries.
▶ Using a #18 Chenille needle and Rousseau Soft Cotton, stitch a **Backstitch** (page 34) over all of the chalk lines.
▶ Using #8 EZM12, stitch a **Closed Tete de Boeuf Stitch** (page 135) down the Avocado grunge main stem.

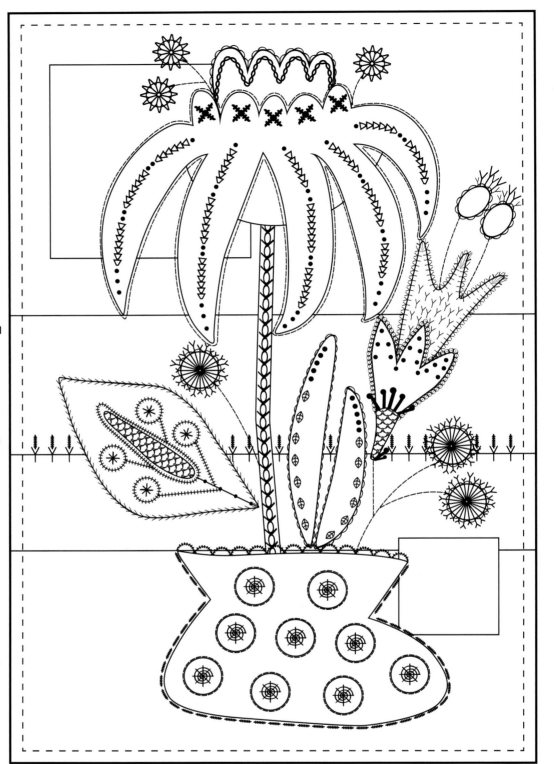

Leaves:

▶ Using #8 EZM95, stitch a **Chain Stitch** (page 169) around the outer edge of the Blue Spruce leaves.
▶ Referring to the diagram, use a #3 Milliners needle and #8 EZM81 stitch five **French Knots** (page 104) at the top of each Blue Spruce leaf. Continue down the leaf using a #3 Milliners

needle and #8 EZM81, stitch **Double Cast Ons** (page 96) until you reach the bottom of the leaf.

▶ Using the diagram provided, draw chalk lines connecting the center Blue Spruce accent to the main stem and the four Blue Spruce circles to the center accent and center chalk line.

▶ Using a #18 Chenille needle and Grandma Moses #3 Painters Thread, stitch a **Palestrina Knot** (page 68) on the chalk line from the accent to the main stem.

▶ Using Grandma Moses #3 Painters Thread with a #18 Chenille needle as the thread to lay down and #8 EZM95 as the couching thread, **Couch** (page 45) over the chalk lines, then around the Blue Spruce center accent, the four circles, and the chalk lines connecting the berries.

▶ Using #8 EZM81, stitch a **Closed Fly Stitch** (page 58) around the outer edge of the cotton Avocado leaf.

▶ Using #8 EZM81, stitch a **Backstitch** (page 34) following the shape of the center accent an ⅛" in from the outer edge. Using #8 EZM81, stitch an **Open Buttonhole Filler Stitch** (page 141) weaving your outer edges through the Backstitch (page 141).

▶ Referring to the diagram, use #8 EZM81 to stitch four ¼" straight stitches to form a star on each ½" Blue Spruce circle.

Berries:

▶ Using #8 EZM99, stitch a **Chain Stitch** (page 169) around the outer edge of the three Raspberry berries.

▶ Using #8 EZM99, stitch random length small **Fly Stitches** (page 127) around the Raspberry circles, finishing each fly stitch in the center of the circle.

Main Flower:

▶ Using #8 EZM19, stitch a **Chain Stitch** (page 169) around the outer edge of the Sea Spray center of the flower, followed by a second row a ¼" in from the edge.

▶ Using a #18 Chenille needle and Silken Pearl Tuscan Sun, stitch a **Backstitch** (page 34) around the outer edge of the Pumpkin flower.

▶ Using a #1 Milliners needle and RZ3130, stitch two **Bullion Knots** (page 92) a ½" long to form a X in each scallop of the Pumpkin flower. *Note: The first Bullion Knot has 16 wraps and the overlapping Bullion Knot has 18 wraps.*

▶ Using #18 Chenille needle and #5 EZM82, stitch **Fly Stitches** (page 127) around the Sun Yellow berries, finishing each fly stitch in the center of the circle.

▶ Referring to the diagram, draw three ⅞" chalk lines down the center of the first four Pumpkin petals and two ⅞" chalk lines down the center of the last Pumpkin petal, leaving a ¼" in between each line.

▶ Using a #1 Milliners needle and #5 EZM82 on petals 1, 2, 3 and 5 stitch a narrow **Van Dyke Stitch** (page 87) on each ⅞" chalk line.

▶ Using a #1 Milliners needle and #3 EZM101 on petal 4 stitch a narrow **Van Dyke Stitch** (page 87) on each ⅞" chalk line. *Note: The horizontal stitches are shortened to a ⅛" to form a braided stitch and use the back of your needle to slide under the crossed threads in the center.*

▶ Referring to the diagram, use a #3 Milliners needle and #8 EZM19 to stitch **French Knots** (page 104) to connect the Van Dyke Stitches.

Small Flower:

▶ Using #8 EZM14, stitch a **Fly Stitch** (page 127) around the outer edge of the Sea Spray grunge flower.

▶ Using #8 EZM14, stitch rows of individual **Fly Stitches** (page 127) on top of the Sea Spray grunge fabric flower.
▶ Using #8 EZM99, stitch a **Chain Stitch** (page 169) around the outer edge of the two Kumquat berries.
▶ Using #8 EZM99, stitch six to seven random length small **Fly Stitches** (page 127) on the top of each Kumquat berry.
▶ Using a #18 Chenille needle and Rousseau Soft Cotton, stitch a **Backstitch** (page 34) around the Peridot base.
▶ Using a #18 Chenille needle and Rousseau Soft Cotton, stitch a horizontal row of **Backstitches** (page 34) one inch above the base of the Peridot section of the flower.
▶ Referring to the diagram, use Rousseau Soft Cotton to stitch an **Open Buttonhole Filler Stitch** (page 141) at the base of the flower, weaving the upper and outer edges through the Backstitch.
▶ Using the back of a #1 Milliners needle or Tapestry needle and Rousseau Soft Cotton, weave a **Pekinese Stitch** (page 40) through the remaining backstitch on the upper part of the Peridot flower.
▶ Using a #1 Milliners needle and Rousseau Soft Cotton, stitch **French Knots** (page 104) along the inside edge of the top of the base of the flower.
▶ Using a #1 Milliners needle and Rousseau Soft Cotton, stitch five **Pistil Stitches** (page 106) along the top edge of the Open Buttonhole Filler Stitch and two at the top of the stem.

Vase:

▶ Using a #3 Milliners needle and #8 EZM36, stitch **Bullion Knots** (page 92) around the outer edge of the Lavender vase excluding the top edge.
▶ Using a #3 Milliners needle and #8 EZM36, stitch **Cast On Bullion Knots** (page 164) on the top edge of the Lavender vase.
▶ Using your circle template and chalk pencil, draw a ½" circle in each of your ¾" Deep Teal circles. Using a #1 Milliners needle and #5 EZ11, stitch a **Whipped Woven Circle** (page 120) in each chalked circle. *Note:* To weave through the spokes, use the back of your Milliners needle or a Tapestry needle so that you do not stitch through the threads that make up the spokes.
▶ Using #5 EZ11, stitch a **Backstitch** (page 34) around each Deep Teal circle.

Block 8

Finished Size: 10" x 15" + ¼" Seam Allowance

Appliqué Threads:

Ellana Wool Thread:
- **EN12** Avocado
- **EN18** Lagoon
- **EN33** Goldenrod
- **EN34** Sun Yellow
- **EN40** Blue Iris
- **EN49** Kumquat
- **EN58** Lavender

Efina Cotton Thread:
- **EF04** Grey Flannel
- **EF10** Spring Leaf
- **EF30** Black
- **EF41** Flame
- **EF54** Powder Blue

Embellishment Threads:

Eleganza Perle Cotton:
- #8 **EZ04** Manatee
- #8 **EZ51** Sortie Cap
- #8 **EZM04** Carbon
- #8 **EZM12** Inchworm
- #8 **EZM14** Lettuce Wrap
- #8 **EZM19** Island Oasis
- #8 **EZM25** Clambake
- #8 **EZM36** Plush Lilac
- #8 **EZM95** Battlefield
- #8 **EZM99** Treasure Your Chest
- #5 **EZM31** Hibiscus
- #5 **EZM82** Haymaker's Punch
- #5 **EZM87** Heard it Through the Grapevine
- #3 **EZ30** After Dinner Mint
- #3 **EZM101** Fight Like a Girl

Other Threads:
Painter's Thread Soft Cotton Rousseau

Background Fabrics:

Hand Dyed Wool:
- Plaid Black Wool
- Solid Black Wool

Cottons & More:
- Black Australian Words
- Grey Silver Metallic

Appliqué:

Hand Dyed Wool:
- Kumquat
- Goldenrod
- Blue Iris
- Lagoon
- Lavender
- Avocado
- Sun Yellow

Cottons & More:
- Black with Button Flowers
- Turquoise & White Leaves on Spring Leaf
- Winter Strata Stripes
- $\frac{5}{16}$" wide Lagoon Rick Rack
- Ribbon Floss Cotton Turner

Background Assembly:

Background:

Cut: Black Plaid wool - 8-½" x 10-½" (A)
Black Solid wool - 7-½" x 10-½" (B)

Sew A to B using a ¼" seam allowance, press the seams open.

Background Layering:

Cut: Black Australian Words Cotton - 4-½" x 4-½"
Grey Silver Metallic Fabric - 3" x 6"

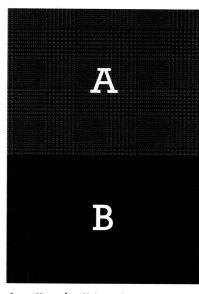

Referring to the photograph, pin the two background pieces in place. Appliqué all background layering in place.

Appliqué:

Base of Leaf, Flowers, Berries and Vase:

Trace separately with a pencil on the matte side of your freezer paper the base elements for the leaf, flowers, berries and vase. Cut out the wool appliqué pieces exactly the same size as the template adding a ¼" to the top of the Avocado base of the main flower to tuck under the Lavender flower and for the cotton fabrics add a ¼" seam allowance so you can needle turn the fabrics. Using a ½" wool punch, create three ½" Kumquat circles for the small flower. Using a 1-½" wool punch, create two 1-½" Kumquat circles for the stamens. Referring to the photograph, iron the templates to the appropriate color wool and cotton fabrics and cut out the appliqué pieces. Using your small appliqué pins, pin all base layers in place.

Main Stem and Rick Rack Stem:

Make a Knot in the end of your Green Ribbon Floss Cotton. Using a #18 Chenille bring your needle to the front of your work an ⅛" under and slightly left of center at the top of your vase. Pull the thread to the front of your work so that the knot anchors the thread in the back, remove your needle. As this is a self ruching thread, you will pull one of the threads from the loose end of the ribbon and draw it up so that the tape ruches up until it measures 3-½" long. Vertically lay the ruched tape on your background to form the main stem. Manipulate the ruching so that the stem is even throughout and pin in place. Pin the rick rack stem in place on the left hand side, tucking the end under the Green Ribbon Floss Cotton. Hand stitch the rick rack in place. Using a #1 Milliners needle and Rousseau Soft Cotton attach the tape to the background using two wrap **French Knots** (page 104). Appliqué all base layers in place. Appliqué the Red/Pink Flower cotton fabric and Avocado base in place before appliquéing the Lavender flower in place.

Layering of the Leaf and Main Flower:

For the layering of the leaf cut out your freezer paper template for the cotton overlay, cut, pin and appliqué in place. For the layering of the main flower cut out your freezer paper templates for the cotton and wool overlays. Cut, pin and appliqué overlays in place.

Bird:

Wait to appliqué and embellish these block-overlapping birds until you begin block assembly.

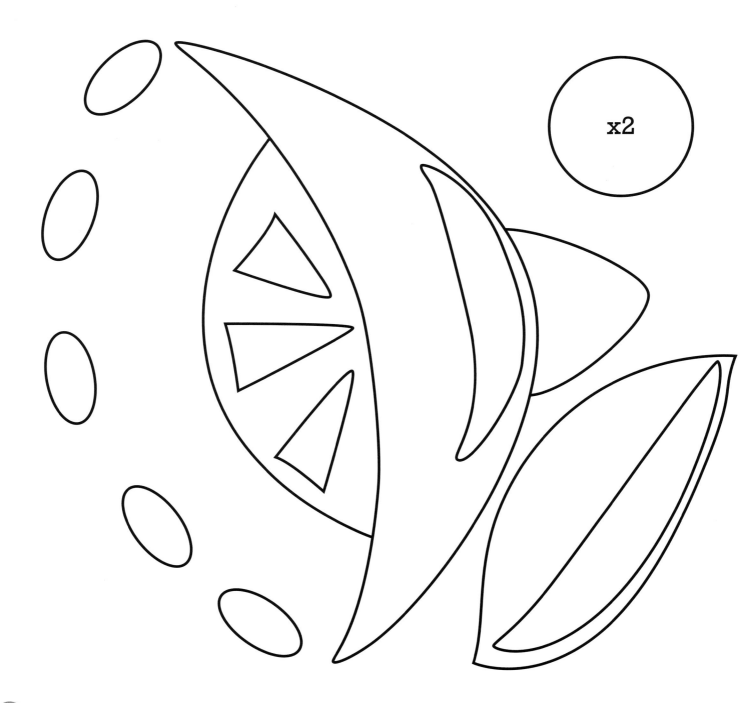

Embellish:

Background:

▶ Using #8 EZM04, stitch small **Running Stitches** (page 26) through the rows of words.

▶ Using #8 EZ04, stitch +'s randomly throughout the Silver Metallic fabric. *Note: This is the last stitch I did on the block, as I worked it around the flower stems and stamens.*

Stems:

▶ Using the diagram provided, draw chalk lines connecting the oval Avocado stamens to the main flower, the ½" Kumquat berries to the Goldenrod flower and the 1-½" Kumquat berries to the main stem. Referring to the diagram, draw four curved chalk lines at the base of the Goldenrod flower.

▶ Using a #18 Chenille needle and Rousseau Soft Cotton, stitch a **Backstitch** (page 34) on the chalk lines connecting the Avocado stamens to the main flower and around each oval Avocado stamen.

▶ Using #8 EZM14, stitch a **Palestrina Knot** (page 68) connecting the ½" Kumquat stamens to the Goldenrod flower.

▶ Using #8 EZM12 with a #24 Chenille needle as the thread to lay down and as the couching thread, **Couch** (page 45) over the four chalk lines at the base of the Goldenrod flower.

▶ Using a #18 Chenille needle and Rousseau Soft Cotton, stitch a **Pekinese Stitch** (page 40) connecting the 1-½" Kumquat berries to the main stem.

▶ Using #8 EZM95, stitch a **Running Stitch** (page 26) through the center of the rick rack stem following the curve of the rick rack.

Leaf:

▶ Using a #3 Milliners needle and #8 EZM95, stitch **Bullion Knots** (page 92) along the bottom edge of the leaf.
▶ Using #8 EZM95, stitch a **Closed Fly Stitch** (page 58) around the top edge of the leaf.
▶ Using a #3 Milliners needle and #8 EZM12, stitch a row of short **Pistil Stitches** (page 106) an ⅛" apart in the center two inches of the leaf overlay.
▶ Referring to the diagram, use #8 EZM36 to stitch random height Straight Stitches with Cross Stitches at the top of the cotton overlay between the Pistil Stitches.

Berries:

▶ Using a #18 Chenille needle and #5 EZM31, stitch a **Fly Stitches** (page 127) around the outer edge of the two Kumquat 1-½" berries.
▶ Draw a one inch chalk circle in the center of the Kumquat berries. Using the edge of the circle as the guide for the V, stitch **Fly Stitches** (page 127) around the circle with the tail finishing in the center of the Kumquat berry.

Main Flower:

▶ Referring to the diagram, draw seven chalk lines through the Avocado base.
▶ Using a #18 Chenille needle and #3 EZ30, stitch a **Split Stitch** (page 79) on each chalk line and around the outer edge of the Avocado base.
▶ Using #8 EZM36, stitch a **Chain Stitch** (page 169) around the Lavender flower.
▶ Using #8 EZM36, stitch a **Running Stitch** (page 26) vertically through the lines in the striped overlay.
▶ Using #8 EZM36, stitch a **Backstitch** (page 34) around the striped overlay.
▶ Using #8 EZM36, stitch Cross Stitches randomly throughout the Lavender flower.
▶ Using a #18 Chenille needle and #5 EZM31, stitch a **Backstitch** (page 34) around the three Sun Yellow accents and random **Detached Chain Stitches** (page 52) throughout the Sun Yellow accents.
▶ Using #8 EZM99, stitch a **Fly Stitch** (page 127) along the top edge followed by rows of Fly Stitches throughout the cotton of the main flower.
▶ Using a #3 Milliners needle and #8 EZ51, stitch two wrap **French Knots** (page 104) in between each row of Split Stitches on the top edge of the Avocado base.
▶ Using a #3 Milliners needle and #8 EZ51, stitch a horizontal ½" long **Double Cast On Stitch** (page 96) using approximately twenty six Cast On Stitches in each oval Avocado stamen.

Small Flower:

▶ Using #5 EZM82 with a #18 Chenille needle as the thread to lay down and #8 EZM25 as the couching thread, **Couch** (page 45) around the Goldenrod flower.
▶ Using #8 EZM25, stitch a **Chain Stitch** (page 169) around the three ½" Kumquat stamens.
▶ Using a #3 Milliners needle and #8 EZM25, stitch a cluster of **French Knots** (page 104) in the center of each Kumquat stamen.
▶ Using a #15 Milliners needle and #3 EZM101, stitch three wrap **French Knots** (page 104) at the end of each curved couched line at the base of the Goldenrod flower.
▶ Using #8 EZM95, stitch a **Backstitch** (page 34) in a semi circle at the base of the Goldenrod flower.

▶ Using #8 EZM95, stitch an **Open Buttonhole Filler Stitch** (page 141) throughout the semicircle.
▶ Referring to the diagram, use #8 EZM19 to stitch a **Fly Stitch** (page 127) at the base of each petal bringing the tail down to the edge of the Open Button Filler semicircle.
▶ Using a #3 Milliners needle and #8 EZM99, stitch a **Bullion Knot** (page 92) in each V of the fly stitch followed by a two wrap **French Knot** (page 104) ⅛" above the Bullion Knot.
▶ Using a #3 Milliners needle and #8 EZ51, stitch a two wrap **French Knot** (page 104) ⅛" above the #8 EZM99 French Knot.

Vase:

▶ Using #5 EZM87 with a #18 Chenille needle as the thread to lay down and as the couching thread, **Couch** (page 45) around the Blue Iris vase.
▶ Referring to the diagram, draw three rows of vertical chalk lines and two rows of horizontal chalk lines.
▶ Using a #1 Milliners needle and #5 EZM87, stitch **Double Cast On Stitches** (page 96) on each chalk line.

Block 9
Finished Size: 12" x 17" + ¼" Seam Allowance

Appliqué Threads:

Ellana Wool Thread:
EN07 Oceanfront
EN10 Spring Leaf
EN13 Electric Lime
EN23 Flamingo
EN25 Salmon
EN34 Sun Yellow
EN46 Mango
EN57 Larkspur
EN58 Lavender

Efina Cotton Thread:
EF04 Grey Flannel
EF10 Spring Leaf
EF12 Avocado
EF14 Peridot
EF18 Lagoon
EF19 Sea Spray
EF30 Black

Embellishment Threads:

Eleganza Perle Cotton:

#8 EZ04 Manatee
#8 EZ51 Sortie Cap
#8 EZM04 Carbon
#8 EZM12 Inchworm
#8 EZM14 Lettuce Wrap
#8 EZM19 Island Oasis
#8 EZM25 Clambake
#8 EZM36 Plush Lilac
#8 EZM81 Victory Bell

#8 EZM99 Treasure Your Chest
#5 EZ06 Snow Globe
#5 EZ52 Love-Lies-Bleeding
#5 EZM82 Haymaker's Punch
#5 EZM87 Heard it Through the Grapevine
#3 EZ30 After Dinner Mint
#3 EZM07 Bee Pollen
#3 EZM13 Over the Clover

Other Threads:
Painter's Thread #3 Perle Cotton Grandma Moses

Background Fabrics:

Hand Dyed Wool:
Solid Black Wool
Check Black Wool

Cottons & More:
Black Dash
Soft Grey Texture
Bees on Black

Appliqué:

Hand Dyed Wool:
Oceanfront
Electric Lime
Flamingo
Larkspur
Lavender
Mango
Salmon
Spring Leaf
Sun Yellow

Cottons & More:
Sea Spray Grunge
Turquoise & White Leaves on Spring Leaf
Avocado Grunge
⅜" wide Lime Green Purple Arrows
3/16" wide Avocado Rick Rack
5/16" wide Lagoon Rick Rack

Background Assembly:

Background:

    Cut: Solid Black Wool - 12-½" x 7-½" (A)
                 Check Black Wool - 12-½" x 10-½" (B)

Sew A to B using a ¼" seam allowance, press the seams open.

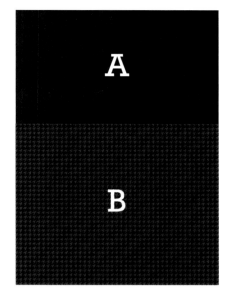

Background Layering:

    Cut: Black Dash Cotton - 1-¾" x 5-¼"
                 Soft Grey Texture Cotton- 4" x 7-½"
                 Bee Print Cotton - 8" x 2"

Referring to the photograph, pin the three background pieces in place. First, appliqué in place the Black Dash and Soft Grey Texture fabrics. Finish by appliquéing the Bee fabric in place, overlapping the Soft Grey Texture.

Appliqué:

Stems:

Pin and appliqué in place the Lime Green and Purple Arrows ribbon main stem. Cut the ³⁄₁₆" wide Avocado Rick Rack into a 4" piece for the left hand stem and a 5" piece for the right hand stem, then pin and appliqué into place.

Base of Leaves, Flowers, Berries and Vase:

Trace separately with a pencil on the matte side of your freezer paper the base elements for the leaves, base of the center flower, left hand flower, berries and vase. Cut out the wool appliqué pieces exactly the same size as the template.

Main Flower:

Using a 1" wool punch, create six 1" Mango circles. Using a ¼" punch, create eighteen ¼" Mango circles.

Left Hand Flower:

Using a ½" wool punch, create five ½" Oceanfront circles. Using a 1" punch, create two 1" Sun Yellow berries.

Right Hand Flower:

Using a ⅜" wool punch, create sixteen ⅜" Larkspur circles. Using a ½" wool punch, create four ½" Flamingo berries. Referring to the photograph, iron the templates to the appropriate color wool and cut out appliqué pieces. Using your small appliqué pins, pin and appliqué all base layers in place except the Sun Yellow berry on the left hand side which will overlap the blocks when pieced together (please keep in a safe place for appliquéing on once blocks are together).

Layering of the Leaves and Left Hand Flower:

For the layering of the leaves, cut out your freezer paper template for the cotton overlay, then cut, pin, and appliqué in place. For the layering of the left hand flower cut out your freezer paper templates for the cotton and wool overlays. Cut, pin, and appliqué overlays in place.

Bird:

Wait to appliqué and embellish these block-overlapping birds until you begin block assembly.

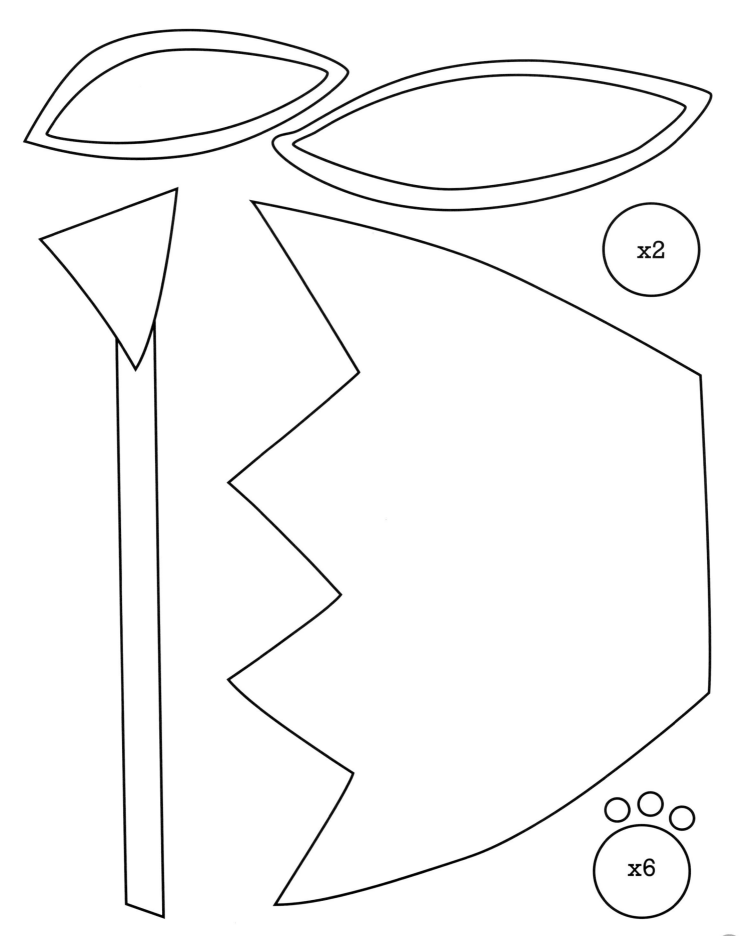

Embellish:

Background:

▶ Using #8 EZM04, stitch small **Running Stitches** (page 26) through the center of the white dash of the Black Dash fabric.

▶ Using #8 EZ04, stitch + randomly through the Soft Grey Texture. *Note: This is the last stitch I did on the block, as I worked it around the main and right hand flowers.*

Stems:

▶ Using the diagram provided, draw chalk lines connecting the 1" Mango circles to the base of the main flower, the ½" Oceanfront circles to the left hand flower, fifteen ⅜" Larkspur circles to the center Larkspur circle on the right hand flower, the ½" Flamingo berries to the right-hand rick rack stem and the 1" Sun Yellow berries to the left hand rick rack stem.

▶ Using #3 EZM07 with a #18 Chenille needle as the thread to lay down and #8 EZM81 as the couching thread, **Couch** (page 45) over the six chalk lines connecting the Mango circles to the main flower and around the outer edge of the Lavender base, adding three vertical lines through the Lavender base.

▶ Using #3 EZ30 with a #18 Chenille needle as the thread to lay down and #8 EZM12 as the couching thread, **Couch** (page 45) the four Oceanfront circles to the left hand flower, the Sun Yellow circles to the left hand rick rack stem, the fifteen circles connecting the right hand flower, and the flamingo berries to the right hand rick rack.

▶ Using #8 EZM81, stitch a **Backstitch** (page 34) on either side of the Lime Green and Purple Arrow main stem.

▶ Using #8 EZM14, stitch two wrap **French Knots** (page 104) on each hill of the two green rick rack stems.

Leaves:

► Using a #18 Chenille needle and #3 EZ30, stitch a **Backstitch** (page 34) around the outer edge of the leaves attached to the main stem.
► Using a #18 Chenille needle and #3 EZM13, stitch a **Closed Fly Stitch** (page 58) throughout the cotton overlay on the leaves attached to the main flower.
► Using #8 EZM12, **Couch** (page 45) over the Closed Fly Stitch to add texture and secure the long fly stitches in place.
► Using a #3 Milliners needles and #8 EZM14 stitch ten wrap **Bullion Knots** (page 92) around the leaves connected to the rick rack stems.

Main Flower:

► Referring to the diagram, use a #1 Milliners needle and #5 EZ06 to stitch a mass of two wrap **French Knots** (page 104) at the base of the flower.
► Draw a ⅝" chalk circle in the center of each 1" Mango circle. Using a #1 Milliners needle and #5 EZM87, stitch a three round ⅝" **Whipped Woven Circles** (page 120) in the center of each Mango circle.
► Using a #18 Chenille needle and #5 EZM87, stitch a **Backstitch** (page 34) around the six 1" Mango circles and the eighteen ¼" Mango circles.
► Using a #3 Milliners needle and #8 EZ51, stitch four vertical rows of four two-wrap **French Knots** (page 104) on the Lavender flower base.

Left Hand Flower:

► Using #8 EZM19, stitch **Fly Stitches** (page 127) around the outer edge of all five Oceanfront circles, finishing the Fly Stitch in the center of the circle.
► Using a #1 Long Darner needle as the anchor needle and a Tapestry needle (or the back of a #15 Milliners needle) for the weaving and #3 EZM13, stitch four five spoke **Woven Picots** (page 148) on the base of the left hand flower. Referring to the diagram, to form each picot place your anchor needle starting 1-¾" out from the base of the flower. *Note: As this is a detached Woven Picot you will need to use one strand of thread to complete each picot. I suggest you cut approximately two yards of thread to make each picot. To attach the picot to the background, I tucked them up a bit to give them dimension.*
► Using a #3 Milliners needle and #8 EZM25, stitch a ten wrap **Bullion Knot** (page 92) vertically at the center point to attach it to the background, followed by one ten wrap **Bullion Knot** (page 92) on either side of the anchor Bullion.
► Using a #3 Milliners needle and #8 EZM25, stitch two twelve wrap **Bullion Knots** (page 92) horizontally, above the vertical Bullion Knots to finish.
► Using a #18 Chenille needle and #5 EZ52, randomly stitch **Detached Chain Stitches** (page 52) throughout the flower, making them a little more concentrated at the top.
► Using a #3 Milliners needle and #8 EZ51, stitch two wrap **French Knots** (page 104) in the center of each Chain Stitch in the top section of the flower, followed by a concentrated area of **French Knots** (page 104) covering the top third of that section.
► Using a #3 Milliners needle and #8 EZM36, stitch two wrap **French Knots** (page 104) in the center of each Chain Stitch in the middle and bottom sections of the flower.
► Using a #15 Milliners needle and #3 EZM13, stitch three ten cast on **Double Cast Ons** (page 96) in the top overlay and four in the bottom overlay.
► Using #8 EZM25, stitch a **Chain Stitch** (page 169) around the outer edge of the Salmon

section of the flower.
- ▶ Using #8 EZM19, stitch a **Chain Stitch** (page 169) around the outer edge of the Larkspur base of the flower and small **Cross Stitches** throughout the Larkspur base.

Right Hand Flower:

- ▶ Using #8 EZM36, stitch an **Eyelet Wheel** (page 112) around all sixteen Larkspur circles starting the eyelet wheel on the outer edge of the circle.
- ▶ Using a #1 Milliners needle and #5 EZ06, stitch random one wrap **French Knots** (page 104) radiating out from the center of the flower.
- ▶ Using #8 EZM99, stitch a **Chain Stitch** (page 169) around the outer edge of the four Flamingo berries.
- ▶ Referring to the diagram, use a #3 Milliners needle and #8 EZM25 to stitch five **Pistil Stitches** (page 106) coming out of the top of each Flamingo berry.
- ▶ Using #3 Milliners needle and #8 EZM19, stitch five two wrap **French Knots** (page 104) at the base of each of the sets of Pistil Stitches.
- ▶ Referring to the diagram, use #8 EZM14 to stitch a Detached **Chain Stitch** (page 169) between each Flamingo berry on either side.

Berries:

- ▶ Using a #18 Chenille for the backstitch, and either the back of a #1 Milliners needle or Tapestry Needle for the stitch, and #5 EZM82, stitch a six round **Trellis Stitch** (page 114) starting on the outer edge of the Sun Yellow berry. Finish with a seventh round using #5 EZM52. *Note: Once you have sewn your blocks together you will repeat the same stitch on the other Sun Yellow berry.*

Vase:

- ▶ Cut the Lagoon rick rack into 3 equal pieces. Referring to the diagram, appliqué the Lagoon rick rack to the vase.
- ▶ Using #3 Painter's Thread Grandma Moses with a #18 Chenille needle as the thread to lay down and as the couching thread, **Couch** (page 45) around the outer edge of the vase.
- ▶ Using #8 EZM14, stitch two wrap **French Knots** (page 104) in each valley of the Lagoon Rick Rack.
- ▶ Referring to the diagram, use a #1 Milliners needle and #3 Painter's Thread Grandma Moses to stitch three vertical ¾" **Needle Weave Bars** (page 166) down the center of the four sections of the vase.

Block 10
Finished Size: 11" x 18" + ¼" Seam Allowance

Appliqué Threads:

Ellana Wool Thread:
EN24 Primrose
EN08 Turquoise
EN13 Electric Lime
EN18 Lagoon
EN20 Cloud
EN23 Flamingo
EN33 Goldenrod
EN40 Blue Iris
EN47 Pumpkin
EN48 Persimmon
EN54 Powder Blue
EN59 Dogwood Rose

Efina Cotton Thread:
EF12 Avocado
EF14 Peridot
EF16 Pine Needle
EF20 Cloud
EF30 Black
EF36 Orchid
EF41 Flame
EF58 Lavender

Embellishment Threads:

Eleganza Perle Cotton:
#8 **EZ51** Sortie Cap
#8 **EZ52** Love-Lies-Bleeding
#8 **EZM04** Carbon
#8 **EZM12** Inchworm
#8 **EZM14** Lettuce Wrap
#8 **EZM19** Island Oasis
#8 **EZM25** Clambake
#5 **EZM82** Haymaker's Punch
#5 **EZM93** Marsh Grass
#5 **EZM97** Navy Jack
#5 **EZM100** Picking up the Pieces
#5 **EZM102** Wild Currant
#3 **EZM13** Over the Clover

Other Threads:
Dazzle DZ1113 Survivor
Razzle RZM19 Pink Warrior

Background Fabrics:

Hand Dyed Wool:
Plaid Black Wool
Solid Black Wool
Check Black Wool

Cottons & More:
Black Mini Polka Dot
Hill Dash on Black
Bees on Black
½" Black Rick Rack

Appliqué:

Hand Dyed Wool:
Blue Iris
Powder Blue
Primrose
Turquoise
Cloud
Lagoon
Goldenrod
Dogwood Rose
Flamingo
Pumpkin
Persimmon
Electric Lime

Cottons & More:
Green Oriental Trees
Green Stripe
Red Grunge
White Dot on Blue
Purple Ferns
¼" wide Lavender Rick Rack
¼" Artichoke Heart Rick Rack

Background Assembly:

Background:

Cut: Plaid Black Wool - 2-½" x 6" (A)
Solid Black Wool - 9-½" x 6" (B)
Check Black Wool - 11-½" x 13" (C)

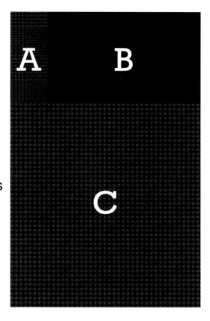

Sew A to B and AB to C using a ¼" seam allowance, press the seams open.

Background Layering:

Cut: Bees on Black Cotton - 5-½" x 5-½" Circle
Hill Dash on Black Cotton - 2-½" x 2-½"
Black Mini Polka Dot Cotton - 4-¾" x 3"
Black Rick Rack - 4-¼"

Referring to the photograph, pin and appliqué the three background pieces in place. Pin and appliqué the Black rick rack a ½" below the top edge of the Black and White Mini Dot overlay.

Appliqué:

Stems:

Pin in place the ¾" x 4-¼" Oriental Trees fabric for the main stem, tucking the green rick racks underneath. The 2-¼" stem is the upper stem and the 2-½" stem is the lower stem. Pin and appliqué all stems in place.

Base of Leaves, Flowers, Berries, Bird and Vase:

Trace separately with a pencil on the matte side of your freezer paper the base elements for the leaves, base of the center flower, left hand flowers, right hand flower, berries, bird and vase. Cut out the wool appliqué pieces exactly the same size as the template, except adding a ¼" at the base of the five Blue Iris petals so they can be tucked under the Lagoon flower base and a ¼" for the Pumpkin beak. Using a ⅜" wool punch, create four ⅜" Electric Lime circles for the right hand flower. Using a ½" wool punch, create four ½" Persimmon circles for the left hand flowers. Referring to the photograph iron the templates to the appropriate color wool and cut out appliqué pieces. Using your small appliqué pins, pin and appliqué all base layers in place except the Lagoon center of the main flower, which will be sewn once the flower petal cotton overlay is appliquéd down.

Layering of the Flower, Bird, Large Leaves, Right Hand Flower and Vase:

For the layering of the flower, bird, large leaves, right hand flower and vase cut out your freezer paper templates for the cotton overlay, cut, pin and appliqué in place. Using a 1" punch, create seven Turquoise 1" circles for the vase. Using a ¼" punch, create six Lagoon ¼" circles for the leaves. Cut, pin and appliqué overlays in place. Finish by attaching the Lagoon base of the main flower.

Embellish:

Background:

▶ Using #8 EZM04, stitch small **Running Stitches** (page 26) through the center of the white dash of the Black Hill Dash fabric.

▶ Using #8 EZM04, stitch a twelve wrap vertical **Bullion Knot** (page 92) in each of the valleys of the Black rick rack.

Stems:

▶ Using the diagram provided, draw chalk lines connecting the stamens to the main flower, stamens to the right hand and left hand flowers, and the left hand flower to the vase.

▶ Using #8 EZM14, stitch a **Pekinese Stitch** (page 40) on the chalk lines to attach the stamens to the main flower.

▶ Using a #18 Chenille needle and #3 EZM13, stitch a **Palestrina Knot** (page 68) on the chalk lines connecting the left hand flowers to the vase.

▶ Using #8 EZM12 as the thread to lay down and #8 EZM14 as the couching thread, **Couch** (page 45) over the chalk lines connecting the stems to the flowers on the right hand and left hand flowers.

▶ Using a #3 Milliners needle and #8 EZM14, stitch two wrap **French Knots** (page 104) on the hills of the Green rick rack stems.

▶ Referring to the diagram, use a #3 Milliners needle and #8 EZM14 to randomly stitch clusters of **Fly Stitches** (page 127) with **Bullion Knots** (page 92) in the center of each 'V' on the left hand flower stems.

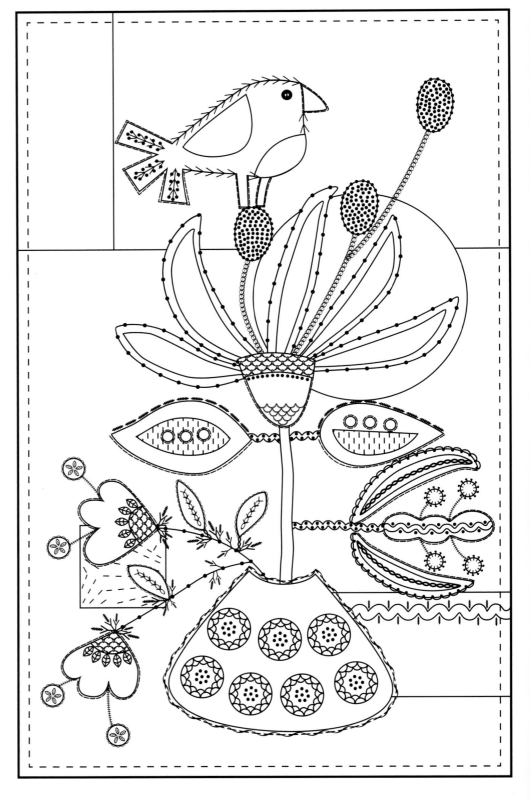

Leaves:

► Using #8 EZM14, stitch a **Chain Stitch** (page 169) around the outer edge of the three small leaves on the left hand flower finishing each leaf by connecting it to the stem.
► Using #8 EZM14, stitch a **Closed Tete de Boeuf** (page 135) down the center of the three small leaves on the left hand flower.
► Using #8 EZM14, stitch vertical lines of **Running Stitches** (page 26) in the center of each stripe on the cotton overlay of the large leaves.
► Using #5 EZM93, stitch a **Backstitch** (page 34) around the ¼" Lagoon circles and the bottom half of each large leaf.
► Using a #1 Milliners needle and #5 EZM93, stitch a row of ten wrap **Bullion Knots** (page 92) on the top edge of the large leaves.

Main Flower:

► Using a #18 Chenille needle and #5 EZM102, stitch a **Palestrina Knot** (page 68) around the edge of all five Blue Iris petals.
► Using a #1 Milliners needle and #5 EZM100, stitch two wrap **French Knots** (page 104) around the outer edge and throughout the three Flamingo stamens.
► Using a #18 Chenille needle and #5 EZM93, stitch a **Backstitch** (page 34) around the outer edge of the Lagoon base of the main flower and a horizontal row a ½" down from the top edge of the Lagoon base.
► Using a #18 Chenille needle and #5 EZM93, fill in the top half inch of the Lagoon base with an **Open Buttonhole Filler Stitch** (page 141) using the Backstitch to weave.
► Referring to the diagram, use a #1 Milliners needle and #5 EZM93 to stitch five horizontal rows of **Cast On Bullion Knots** (page 164), with 12 cast ons, on the Lagoon base.
► Using a #1 Milliners needle and #5 EZM102, stitch a row of one wrap **French Knots** (page 104) along the bottom edge of the Buttonhole Filler Stitch.

Left Hand Flower:

► Coming up 1" from the base of the flower draw a semicircle line.
► Using a #18 Chenille needle and #5 EZM82, stitch a **Backstitch** (page 34) around the outer edge of the Goldenrod flowers and over the chalk line.
► Using a #18 Chenille needle and #5 EZM82, stitch an **Open Buttonhole Filler Stitch** (page 141) for approximately a ½" (about four rows), change to #8 EZM25 and continue the Open Buttonhole Filler Stitch another ¼" (about three rows).
► Using a #3 Milliners needle and #8 EZM19, stitch five small vertical **Double Cast On Stitches** (page 96), with approximately eight cast ons, along the upper edge of the Buttonhole Filler Stitch.
► Using #8 EZM25, stitch a **Chain Stitch** (page 169) around the outer edge of the four Persimmon circles.
► Using #8 EZM25, stitch five **Detached Chain Stitches** (page 52) in the center of the Persimmon circles to form a small flower.

Right Hand Flower:

► Appliqué in place the Lavender rick rack down the center of the Dogwood Rose flower turning under the edges.
► Using #18 Chenille needle and DZ1113, stitch a **Backstitch** (page 34) around the outer edge

of the Dogwood Rose flower.
▶ Using a #3 Milliners needle and #8 EZ51, stitch two wrap **French Knots** (page 104) in each valley of the Lavender rick rack.
▶ Using a #18 Chenille needle and #5 EZ52, stitch a **Backstitch** (page 34) on the inside edge of the Primrose petals.
▶ Using a #18 Chenille needle and #5 EZ52, stitch a **Scroll Stitch** (page 133) on the outer edge of the Primrose petals.
▶ Using RZM19, stitch a **Chain Stitch** (page 169) down the center of the cotton overlay of the Primrose petals.
▶ Using a #3 Milliners needle and #8 EZM14, stitch **Pistil Stitches** (page 106) radiating out from the center of the Electric Lime circles.

Bird:

▶ Using #18 Chenille needle and #5 EZM31, stitch a **Backstitch** (page 34) around the birds beak.
▶ Using Razzle 3130, stitch a **Closed Fly Stitch** (page 58) around the birds body and a **Backstitch** (page 34) around the legs, tail and across the beak.
▶ Using Razzle 3130, stitch a **Closed Fly Stitch** (page 58) through each tail feather.
▶ Using #1 Milliners needle and #5 EZM31, stitch one wrap **French Knots** (page 104) at the end of each point of the Closed Fly Stitch on the tail feathers.

Vase:

▶ Using a #18 Chenille needle and #5 EZM97, stitch a **Threaded Backstitch** (page 37) around the outer edge of the vase.
▶ Using a #18 Chenille needle and #5 EZM97, stitch a four round **Trellis Stitch** (page 114) around each of the overlay circles.
▶ Using a #1 Milliners needle and #5 EZM97, stitch two wrap **French Knots** (page 104) in the center of the circle overlays.

Block 11
Finished Size: 11" x 25" + ¼" Seam Allowance

Appliqué Threads:

Ellana Wool Thread:
EN09 Amazon Green
EN10 Spring Leaf
EN16 Pine Needle
EN18 Lagoon
EN23 Flamingo
EN33 Golden Rod
EN35 Old Gold
EN47 Pumpkin
EN54 Powder Blue

Efina Cotton Thread:
EF04 Grey Flannel
EF06 Charcoal
EF10 Spring Leaf
EF30 Black
EF41 Flame
EF43 Dark Cerise
EF49 Kumquat

Embellishment Threads:

Eleganza Perle Cotton:
#8 EZ04 Manatee
#8 EZM04 Carbon
#8 EZM19 Island Oasis
#8 EZM25 Clambake
#8 EZM81 Victory Bell
#8 EZM95 Battlefield
#8 EZM99 Treasure Your Chest
#5 EZ52 Love-Lies-Bleeding
#5 EZM31 Hibiscus
#5 EZM97 Navy Jack
#5 EZM100 Picking up the Pieces
#3 EZ30 After Dinner Mint
#3 EZM07 Bee Pollen
#3 EZM13 Over the Clover
#3 EZM101 Fight Like a Girl

Other Threads:
Petite Very Velvet Lite Green
Gold Rush 14
Razzle RZM19 Pink Warrior

Background Fabrics:

Hand Dyed Wool:
Solid Black Wool
Textured Black Wool
Plaid Black Wool

Cottons & More:
Black Grunge
Large White Dot on Black
Soft Grey Texture
⅜" Swiss Dot Ribbon

Appliqué:

Hand Dyed Wool:
Pumpkin
Pine Needle
Amazon Green
Old Gold
Spring Leaf
Powder Blue
Flamingo
Cloud

Cottons & More:
Orange Dot
Lime Solid
Turquoise Crosses on Green
Green with Pins
Artichoke Heart Texture
Wine Pods
Red & White Square Cotton
White Squares on Flame
⁵⁄₁₆" wide Black Buttons

Background Assembly:

Background:

Cut: Solid Black Wool - 16" x 11-1½" (A)
Textured Black Wool - 3" x 11-½" (B)
Plaid Black Wool - 7-1/2" x 11-½" (C)

Sew A to B and AB to C using a ¼" seam allowance, press the seams open.

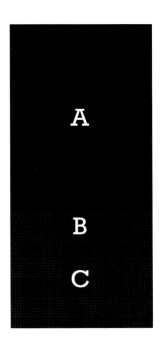

Background Layering:

Cut: Black Grunge Cotton - 10" x 3"
Large White Dot on Black Cotton - 5-1/2" x 5"
Soft Grey Texture Cotton - 5-½" x 4-½"
White Dots on Black Ribbon - 2" and 2-¾"

Referring to the photograph, pin and appliqué the three background pieces in place. Pin and appliqué in place the 2-¾" Black Polka Dot Ribbon 2" from the base of the Soft Grey Texture and the 2" White Dots on Black Ribbon 2-½" from the base for the Soft Grey Texture.

Appliqué:

Stems:

Pin and appliqué in place the ¾" x 7-½" Lime Solid fabric for the main stem.

Base of Leaves, Flower, Berries and Vase:

Trace separately with a pencil on the matte side of your freezer paper the base elements for the leaves, flower, berries and vase. Cut out the wool appliqué pieces exactly the same size as the template, except adding a ¼" to the two Spring Leaf leaves that tuck under the large cotton floral circle. For the center large floral circle trace on heavy duty freezer paper a 5" circle from the pattern provided. Cut it out on the pencil line and iron it to the back of the floral fabric. Cut the fabric out a ¼" larger. With a contrasting color cotton thread stitch a small running stitch in the center of the seam allowance and draw it up so it molds around the freezer paper. Using a ¾" wool punch, create two ¾" Powder Blue circles for the bottom berries connected to base of the stem. Using a 1" wool punch, create two 1" Powder Blue circles for the top berries connected to the base of the stem. Referring to the photograph, iron the templates to the appropriate color wool and cut out appliqué pieces. Using your small appliqué pins, pin and appliqué all base layers in place.

Layering of the Flower, Leaves and Vase:

For the layering of the flower, leaves and vase cut out your freezer paper template for the cotton overlay, cut, pin and appliqué in place. Cut out the wool appliqué pieces exactly the same size as the template. Using a 1" punch, create six Old Gold 1" circles for the main flower. Using a

¼" punch, create seven Amazon Green ¼" circles for the center Old Gold overlay. Cut, pin and appliqué overlays in place.

Bird:

Wait to appliqué and embellish these block-overlapping birds until you begin block assembly.

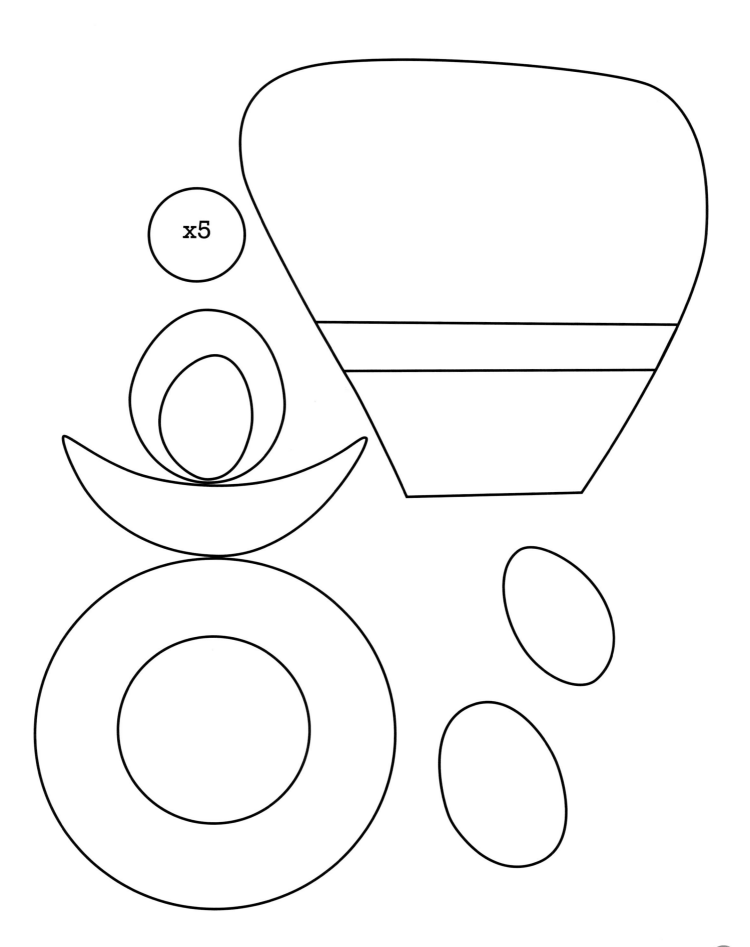

Embellish:

Background:

▶ Using #8 EZM04, stitch a **Running Stitch** (page 26) on the inside edge of each printed white circle.

▶ Referring to the diagram, use #8 EZM04 to stitch two rows of **Fly Stitches** (page 127) at the base of the Soft Grey Texture.

▶ Using a #3 Milliners needle and #8 EZ04, stitch a **Bullion Knot** (page 92) in the center of each 'V' of the Fly Stitches.

▶ Using a #3 Milliners needle and #8 EZ04, stitch **French Knots** (page 104) randomly throughout the Black Grunge.

Stems:

▶ Using the diagram provided, draw chalk lines connecting the Powder Blue oval berries to the main stem, the six leaves to the main stem and the base Powder Blue berries to the main stem.

▶ Using a #18 Chenille needle and #3 EZM13, stitch a **Palestrina Knot** (page 68) on the chalk lines connecting the Powder Blue oval berries to the main stem.

▶ Using a #18 Chenille needle and #3 EZ30, stitch a **Stem Stitch** (page 82) to connect the leaves to the main stem.

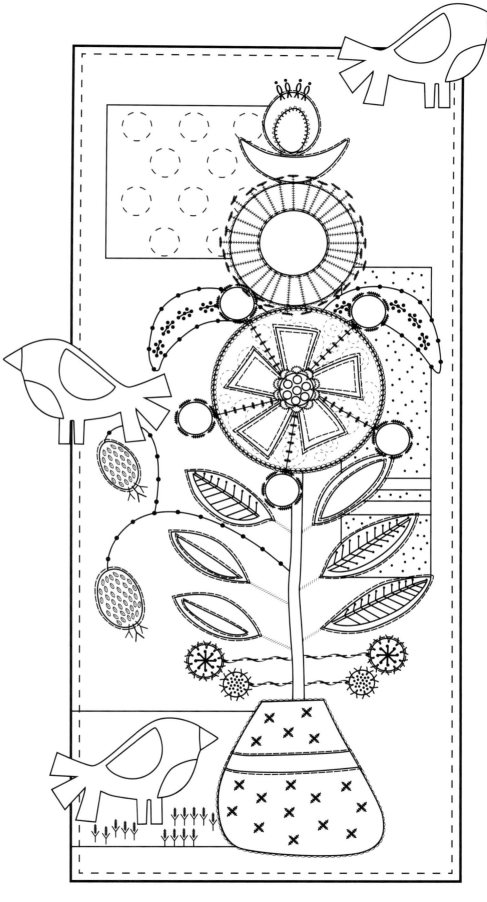

▶ Using a #18 Chenille needle stitch a **Threaded Backstitch** (page 37) using #3 EZ30 as the Backstitch and #3 EZM13 as the weaving thread to connect the Powder Blue circles to the bottom of the main stem.

Leaves:

▶ Using a #18 Chenille needle and Petite Very Velvet, stitch a **Backstitch** (page 34) around the outer edge of all the leaves.
▶ Using a #18 Chenille needle and Petite Very Velvet, stitch a **Backstitch** (page 34) around the outer edge of the overlay of the top right and middle and bottom left leaves.
▶ Using a #18 Chenille needle and Petite Very Velvet, stitch a **Closed Fly Stitch** (page 58) down the center of the top left and middle and bottom right leaves.
▶ Using a #1 Milliners needle and Petite Very Velvet, stitch **French Knots** (page 104) at the ends of each 'V' on the middle right leaf.
▶ Using a #1 Milliners needle and Petite Very Velvet, stitch **French Knots** (page 104) on the top edge of each 'V' on the top left leaf and bottom right leaf.
▶ Using a #18 Chenille needle and Petite Very Velvet, stitch a **Palestrina Knot** (page 104) around the Spring Leaf leaves and down the center of each leaf stitching four ½" Palestrina Knot sections each consisting of three knots.
▶ Using a #3 Milliners needle and #8 EZM95, stitch **French Knots** (page 104) between each of the Palestrina Knots running down the center of the Spring Leaf leaves, repeat on opposite side of the Palestrina Knots.

Main Flower:

▶ Using a #18 Chenille needle and #3 EZM07, stitch a **Backstitch** (page 34) around the outer edge of the Old Gold oval.
▶ Using a #18 Chenille needle and #3 EZM07, stitch four **Tete de Boeufs** (page 135) on the top of the Old Gold oval.
▶ Using a #15 Milliners needle and #3 EZM07, stitch a **French Knot** (page 104) at the end of each Tete de Boeuf stitch.
▶ Using #8 EZM95, stitch an **Italian Knotted Border stitch** (page 62) around the Amazon Green overlay with four **Chain Stitches** (page 169) at the base of the overlay.
▶ Using a #18 Chenille needle and Petite Very Velvet, stitch a **Backstitch** (page 34) around the Spring Leaf crescent shape.
▶ Using #8 EZM95, stitch a **Chain Stitch** (page 169) around the large Amazon Green circle.
▶ Using a #18 Chenille needle stitch a **Pekinese Stitch** (page 40) using Gold Rush 14 as the Backstitch and #5 EZ52 as the weaving thread around the large floral cotton circle.
▶ Using a #3 Milliners needle and #8 EZM81, stitch **Bullion Knots** (page 104) around the five Old Gold 1" berries.
▶ Using a #18 Chenille needle and #3 EZM101, stitch a **Backstitch** (page 34) around the outer edge of the Flamingo overlay and a **Backstitch** (page 34) ¼" inside the Flamingo overlay ¼" from the edge.
▶ Using the diagram provided, draw chalk lines connecting the five Old Gold 1" circles to the sixth center Old Gold 1" circle. Using a #18 Chenille needle and two strands of #3 EZM07 as the thread to lay down and a #3 Milliners needle with #8 EZM81 as the couching thread, **Couch Using Bullion Knots** (page 47) over the chalk lines connecting the five Old Gold berries to the sixth center Old Gold berry.
▶ Using #3 Milliners needle and #8 EZM81, stitch two rows of **Cast On Bullion Knots** (page

164) around the Old Gold 1" center berry.
► Using #8EZM99, stitch **Running Stitches** (page 26) around the burgundy circles of the floral print.
► Using #8 EZM19, stitch **Running Stitches** (page 26) around the turquoise circles of the floral print.
► Using #8 EZM25, stitch **Running Stitches** (page 26) around the orange circles of the floral print.
► Referring to the diagram, use a #18 Chenille needle and #5 EZ52 as the thread to lay down and #8 EZM99 as the couching thread to **Couch** (page 45) radiating lines from the red cotton overlay out past the Amazon Green circle in varying lengths.
► Using a #1 Milliners needle and #5 EZM31, stitch small horizontal **Bullion Knots** (page 92) at the end of each Couched line.
► Using a #18 Chenille needle and #5 EZM31, stitch a **Backstitch** (page 34) around the outer edge of the red cotton overlay.

Berries:

► Using a #18 Chenille needle and #5 EZM97, stitch a **Backstitch** (page 34) around the Powder Blue oval berries on the left hand side.
► Using a #18 Chenille needle and #5 EZM97, stitch three **Fly Stitches** (page 127) at the tip of each Powder Blue oval berry.
► Using a #18 Chenille needle and Gold Rush 14, stitch rows of individual **Chain Stitches** (page 169) throughout the Powder Blue oval berries.
► Using a #18 Chenille needle and #5 EZM100, stitch a **Backstitch** (page 34) around the 1" Powder Blue berries.
► Using a #1 Milliners needle and #5 EZM100, stitch **Pistil Stitches** (page 106) radiating out from the center of the 1" Powder Blue berries.
► Using RZM19, stitch an **Italian Knotted Border Stitch** (page 62) around the 1" Powder Blue berries.
► Using #8 EZM19, stitch an **Italian Knotted Border Stitch** (page 62) around the ¾" Powder Blue berries.
► Using a #1 Milliners needle and #5 EZM97, stitch two wrap **French Knots** (page 104) throughout the Powder Blue ¾" berries.

Vase:

► Using a #1 Milliners needle #5 EZM31, stitch ⅜" **Bullion Knots** (page 92) in the form of X's.
Note: The first Bullion Knot is about 14 wraps and the overlaying Bullion Knot is about 16 wraps.
► Using a #18 Chenille needle and #5 EZM31, stitch a **Backstitch** (page 34) around the cotton overlay and a X in each center circle of the printed fabric.
► Using a #18 Chenille needle and #5 EZM31, stitch a **Chain Stitch** (page 169) around the outer edge of the vase.

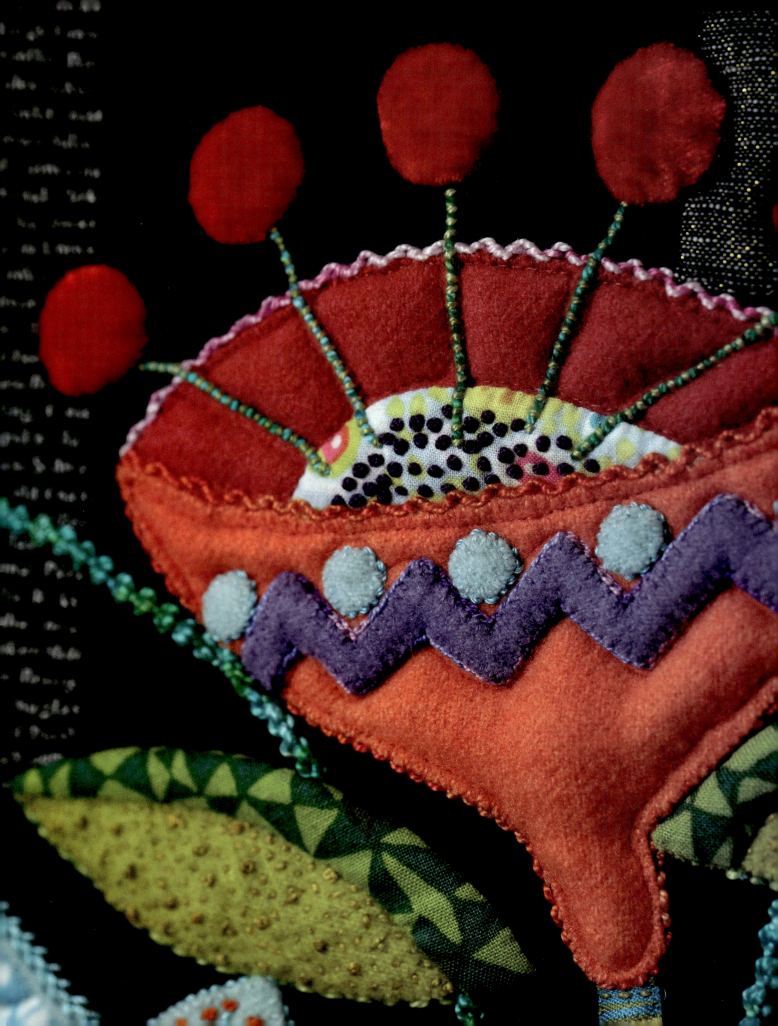

Block Assembly

Finished Size: 43" x 43"

Appliqué Threads:

Ellana Wool Thread:
EN20 Cloud
EN34 Sun Yellow
EN47 Pumpkin

Efina Cotton Thread:
EF20 Cloud

Embellishment Threads:

Eleganza Perle Cotton:
#5 EZ52 Love-Lies-Bleeding
#5 EZM31 Hibiscus
#5 EZM82 Haymaker's Punch

Other Threads:
RZ3130 Aqua Sea

Block Assembly Diagram:

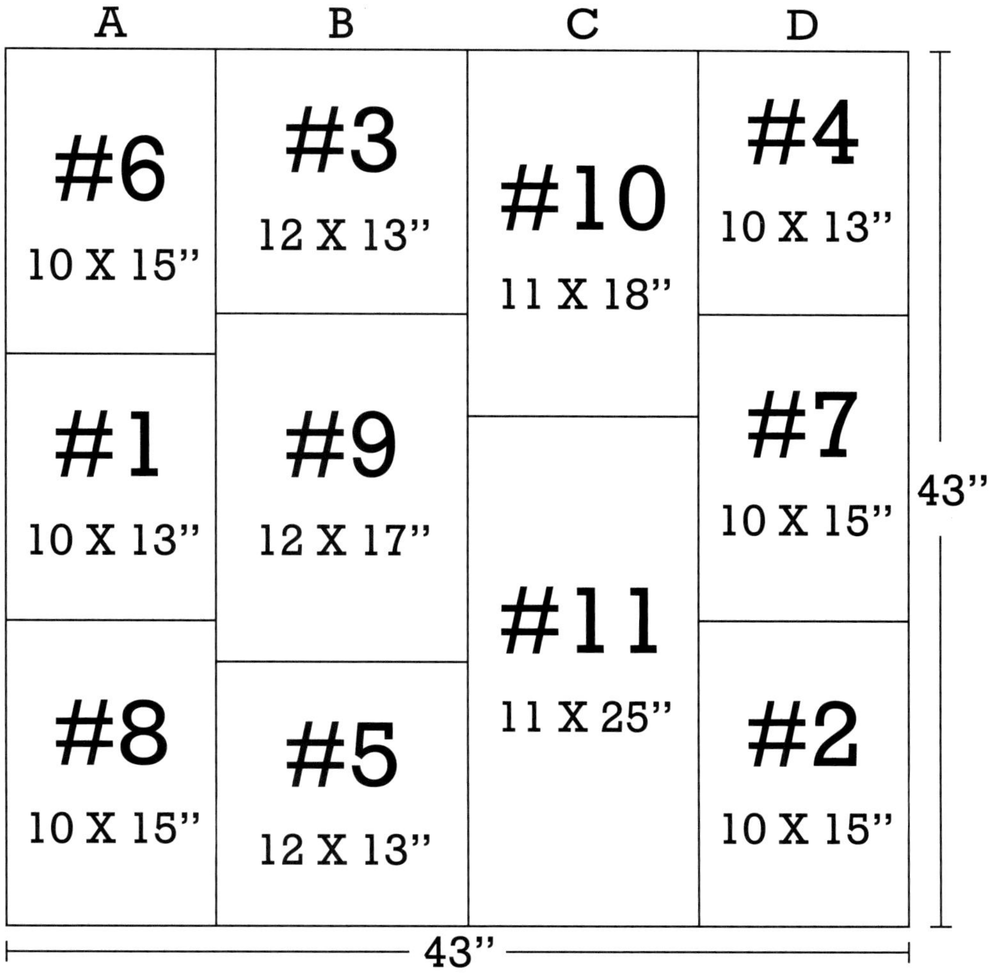

A	B	C	D
#6 10 X 15"	#3 12 X 13"	#10 11 X 18"	#4 10 X 13"
#1 10 X 13"	#9 12 X 17"		#7 10 X 15"
#8 10 X 15"	#5 12 X 13"	#11 11 X 25"	#2 10 X 15"

43" x 43"

Block Assembly:

Background:

▶ Using a ¼" seam allowance throughout and pressing your seams open using a Strip Stick sew Blocks 3, 9 and 5 together, forming panel B.

▶ Sew blocks 10 and 11 together, forming panel C.

▶ Sew panel B to C.

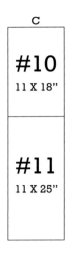

▶ You will now appliqué in place the bird that overlays Blocks 9 and 11, as well as, the bird that overlays Blocks 5 and 11. Refer back to Block 9 and Block 11 for the bird drawings.

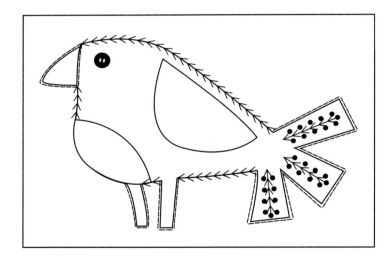

Embellish Bird Overlays:

▶ Using #18 Chenille needle and #5 EZM31 stitch a **Backstitch** (page 34) around the birds beak.
▶ Using Razzle 3130 stitch a **Closed Fly Stitch** (page 58) around the birds body and a **Backstitch** (page 34) around the legs, tail and across the beak.
▶ Using Razzle 3130 stitch a **Closed Fly Stitch** (page 58) through each tail feather.
▶ Using #1 Milliners needle and #5 EZM31 stitch one wrap **French Knot** (page 104) at the end of each point of the Closed Fly Stitch on the tail feathers.
▶ Using #8 EZM04 sew the bird eyes in place.

Final Assembly:

▶ Sew blocks 6, 1 and 8 together, forming panel A.

▶ Sew A to BC.

▶ You will now appliqué in place the bird that overlays Blocks 9 and 1, as well as, the bird that overlays Blocks 8 and 5. Refer back to Block 8 and Block 9 for the bird drawings.

▶ Referring to the diagram and back to Block 9 appliqué in place and embellish the 1" Sun Yellow berry.

▶ Embellish the birds as previously explained.

▶ Sew blocks 4, 7 and 2 together, forming panel D.

▶ Sew D to ABC.

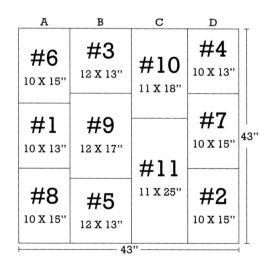

▶ You will now appliqué in place the bird that overlays Blocks 10, 11 and 7. Refer back to Block 11 for the bird drawing.

▶ Embellish the birds as previously explained.

▶ Using #8 EZM04 sew the bird eyes in place on Blocks 3 and 10.

Borders
Finished Size: 49" x 49"

Appliqué Threads:

Efina Cotton Thread:
EF06 Charcoal
EF30 Black

Embellishment Threads:

Eleganza Perle Cotton:
#8 **EZ04** Manatee
#8 **EZM04** Carbon

Other Threads:
Petite Very Velvet Lite Green
Gold Rush 14

Fabrics:

Hand Dyed Wool:
Solid Black Wool

Cottons:
Black Grunge
Black Dash
Black Mini Polka Dot
Soft Grey Texture
Black Australian Words

Background Assembly:

Background:

Cut: Black Solid wool for Left and Right Border - 43-½" x 3-½" (x2)
Black Solid wool for Top and Bottom Border - 49-½" x 3-½" (x2)

Cut two 43-½" x 3-½" black borders and sew to the left and right hand sides of the quilt using a ¼" seam allowance, press seams open. Cut two 49-½" x 3-½" black borders and sew to the top and bottom of the quilt using a ¼" seam allowance, press seams open. **Note:** *With long cuts such as these I always snip and rip the wool- the wool will always rip on a straight line; it is much easier than cutting the strips with a rotary cutter.*

Appliqué:

Cotton Circles:

All circles on the outer border are 2-¾" finished circles. You can either use heavy duty freezer paper or Perfect Circles to make the cotton circles. Cut the circles from the following fabrics:

Five - Black Grunge Cotton (A)
Five - Black Dash Cotton (B)
Four - Black Mini Polka Dot Cotton (C)
Three - Light Grey Texture Cotton (D)
Two - Black Australian Words Cotton (E)

Use the diagram provided to the right for the placement of appliquéd circles.

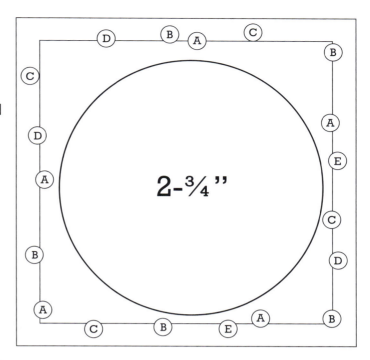

Embellish:

Black Grunge Circles (A):

▶ Referring to the diagram draw four lines ¼" apart forming an 'X'. Using #8 EZ04 stitch a **Running Stitch** (page 26) on all four lines. From the center of the circle draw a 2-½", 1-¾" and 1-¼" circle. Using #8 EZ04 stitch a **Running Stitch** (page 26) on the chalk lines to form three circles.

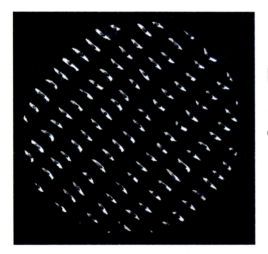

Black Dash Circles (B):

▶ Using #8 EZM04 stitch a **Running Stitch** (page 26) in the center of each dash.

Black Mini Polka Dot Circles (C):

▶ Using #8 EZM04 randomly stitch **Cross Stitches** throughout the circle using the dots as a guide.

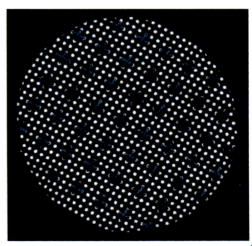

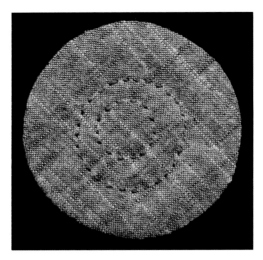

Soft Grey Texture Circles (D):

► Using your circle template draw a 1-¼" circle in the center of your circle then add a ¾" circle within that circle. Using #8 EZ04 stitch a **Running Stitch** (page 26) on your chalk lines.

Black Australian Words Circles (E):

► Using #8 EZM04 stitch rows of horizontal and vertical **Running Stitches** (page 26) in between the rows of writing.

Finishing
Size: 49" x 49"

Backing:

I always love to use fun backs. You will cut the larger backing piece in half vertically along the fold and piece by machine the hand selected strip of fabric to make the quilt backing big enough for your quilt.

Batting:

I like to use Dream Wool batting in my wool quilts. The wool batting quilts beautifully and has a little more loft than the cotton batting. The wool batting is available for sale on the notions page my website. You will need a throw size.

Quilting:

You can either machine or hand quilt your piece. You can also do a combination of machine and hand quilting stitches. If you are machine quilting with your Ellana wool thread I use a #16 Topstitching needle in the machine and regular 50 weight cotton thread in the bobbin. I would stitch around each image and then echo the background incorporating the embroidery into your design. I suggest you do a little machine quilting on the appliqué pieces, but not too much as to distract from your embroidery. In the border I would do a graphic design echoing the circles. Many longarm quilters do a fabulous job quilting on wool. My suggestion would be to ask them to quilt the background fairly tightly which will give you another textured layer on your quilt. I have seen many quilts successfully hand quilted using big stitch quilting and #8 Eleganza Perle Cotton.

Binding:

Cut your black dot fabric for your binding into five 2-½" strips. Join these on the bias and then press in half to form a double binding. This makes a continuous binding that can now be sewn onto your quilt.

Label:

Iron freezer paper to the back of your White Cotton fabric. This helps stabilize it and makes writing easier. Using a lightbox and a 05 Pigma Pen™ trace the label below then personalize with your name, state and town, date and any special message you would like to add. Remove the freezer paper from the back and heat set for 2 minutes with a hot dry iron. Hand sew to the back of your quilt.

English Garden Needle Roll
Finished Size: 16" x 8-½" Open

Appliqué Threads:

Ellana Wool Thread:
- EN07 Oceanfront
- EN08 Turquoise
- EN09 Amazon Green
- EN10 Spring Leaf
- EN14 Peridot
- EN22 Raspberry
- EN37 Very Berry
- EN48 Persimmon
- EN57 Larkspur
- EN59 Dogwood Rose

Efina Cotton Thread:
- EF04 Grey Flannel
- EF05 Slate
- EF08 Turquoise
- EF10 Spring Leaf
- EF19 Sea Spray
- EF32 Golden Wheat
- EF41 Flame
- EF46 Mango
- EF49 Kumquat

Embellishment Threads:

Eleganza Perle Cotton:

#8 EZ05 Black Tie
#8 EZ09 Sea Glass
#8 EZ21 Let's Pink
#8 EZ31 Call-a-treuse
#8 EZM12 Inchworm
#8 EZM14 Lettuce Wrap
#8 EZM20 Riptide
#8 EZM21 Birds Eye View
#8 EZM30 Crushed Clementine

#8 EZM31 Hibiscus
#8 EZM36 Plush Lilac
#5 EZ05 Black Tie
#5 EZ10 Paradise Blue
#5 EZ17 Lion's Mane
#5 EZM20 Riptide
#5 EZM31 Hibiscus
#3 EZ09 Sea Glass

Construction Fabrics:

Hand Dyed Wools:
Charcoal • 6" x 9"
Persimmon • 4" x 11"
Spring Leaf • 9" x 11"

Cottons & More:
Aqua/Yellow Polka Dot • 6" x 11"
Charcoal Linen • 6" x 9"
Charcoal Print • 6" x 5-½"
Charcoal Yarn Dye • ¼ Yard
Turquoise Stripe • Fat ⅛th

Appliqué Fabrics:

Hand Dyed Wools:
Amazon • 1" x 1"
Dogwood Rose • 2" x 2"
Larkspur • ½" x 2-½"
Oceanfront • 1" x 1"
Peridot • 1" x 1"
Persimmon • 1" x 1"
Raspberry • 2" x 2"
Spring Leaf • 1" x 6-½"
Turquoise • 3-½" x 4-½"
Very Berry • 1-½" x 1-½"

Cottons Fabrics:
Turquoise Circle • 5" x 5"
Green Texture • 4" x 1"
Green Solid Stem • 1" x 2-½"
Green Stripe • 2" x 1"
Two Orange Prints • 6" x 6"
Orange Solid • 2" x 4"

Additional Items:
Fiber Filling
Grey Stripe for Binding • ⅛th Yard
Cotton Batting • 18" x 18"

Additional Embellishments:

9" Turquoise Zipper
9" Green Zipper
Large Button • Approximately 1-¾"
Green Elastic • 4-½"
Large Chartreuse Rick-Rack • 9"
⅝" Blue Flower Wheel Ribbon • 27"
⅜" Mint & Mustard Stems Ribbon • 9"
⅝" Circle on Grey Ribbon • 9"

Small Green Rick-Rack • 2"
Medium Green Rick-Rack • 2"
Charcoal Yarn • 18"
¼" Red Buttons • 15 ea
¼" Green Buttons • 3 ea
Orange #8 Seed Beads • 3 ea
⅜" Hexagon Papers • 7 ea
½" Hexagon Papers • 7 ea

Front Assembly:

Background:

Cut:
- (A) Charcoal hand dyed wool - 5-½" x 8 ½"
- (B) Charcoal cotton print for overlay - 5-½" x 3"
- (C) Charcoal yarn dyed fabric - 6" x 8 ½"
- (D) Charcoal linen fabric - 5-½" x 8 ½"
- (E) Aqua/yellow polka dot pocket - 5-½" x 10 ½"
- (F) Charcoal cotton print for pocket overlay - 5-½" x 1-¾"

  Batting cut one piece 16" x 8 ½"

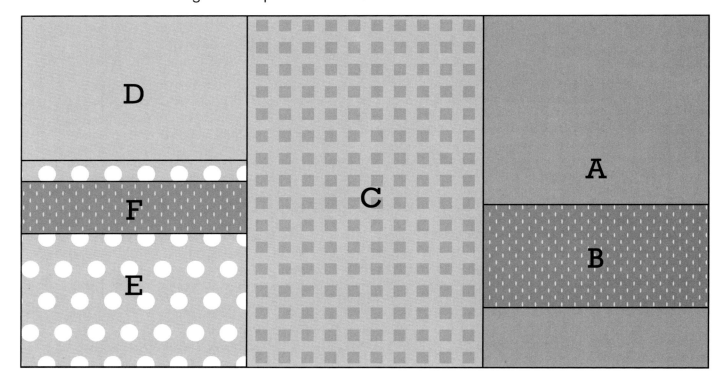

Appliqué:

Appliqué the charcoal cotton print overlay (B) 1-½" up from the bottom edge of (A) the charcoal wool. Couch the Grey yarn along the top and bottom edge of the cotton print overlay.

Freezer Paper Templates:

Trace the pattern pieces for the outside appliqué on the matte side of your freezer paper. Cut out the freezer paper templates. Referring to the photographs press templates with a hot dry iron to the right side of the appropriate wool and cotton color fabrics. Cut out the wool pieces the same size as your freezer paper templates and add a ¼" seam allowance to the cotton appliqué pieces. Hand piece a ⅜" flower hexagon fussy cutting your orange fabrics. Press and remove the papers. For the center stem cut a ¼" green bias strip 2-¼" long. Pin the three flowers, three stems and vase in place. Appliqué these pieces to the background. Pin and appliqué the striped fabric to the base of the vase, flower layers to the three flowers and four leaves and leaf layers in place. With a chalk pencil draw the long stem on the background and stitch a **Palestrina Knot** (page 68) using #8 EZM14 on the line to form a stem. Appliqué the small wool leaves and flower to this stem. For the ¼" wool circles on the center flower you can use a ¼" punch instead of hand cutting these small pieces. For wool appliqué I use a small whipstitch with 50/50 wool thread and a #24 Chenille needle. For needle turn cotton appliqué I use a 60wt cotton thread with #11 Straw needle.

Embellish:

Lilac Flower:

▶ Using #8 EZM36 and a #3 Milliners needle, stitch **Bullion Knots** (page 92) around the outside of the circle and French Knots on the lilac wool.
▶ Using #8 EZM36 and a #24 Chenille needle, stitch a **Backstitch** (page 34) around the flower shape.
▶ Using #8 EZM30 and a #3 Milliners needle, stitch a **Pistil Stitch** (page 106) in each valley of the center flower shape.
▶ Using #5 EZ10 and a #1 Milliners needle, stitch **French Knots** (page 104) around the center of the flower.

Small Orange Flower:

▶ Using #8 EZM31 and a #3 Milliners needle, stitch a row of **Cast On Bullion Stitches** (page 164) around the outer edge of the flower and a second row on the flower.

Hexagon Flower:

▶ Using #5 EZM31 and a #18 Chenille needle, stitch a **Backstitch** (page 34) around each individual hexagon on the flower.
▶ Using #8 EZ09 and a #3 Milliners needle, stitch **Drizzle Stitches** (page 100) in the center of the flower attaching an orange seed bead to the ends of the three center Drizzle Stitches.

Pink Flower:

▶ Using #8 EZ21 and a #24 Chenille needle, stitch a **Chain Stitch** (page 169) around the outer edge of the flower.
▶ Using #5 EZ10 and a #1 Milliners needle, stitch **French Knots** (page 104) around the outer edge of the center circle.
▶ Using #8 EZM36 and a #3 Milliners needle, stitch a circle of **French Knots** (page 104) in the center of the flower.

Leaves and Stems:

► Using #8 EZM21 and a #3 Milliners needle, stitch **French Knots** (page 104) on each hill of the medium rick rack.
► Using #8 EZ31 and a #24 Chenille needle, stitch a **Backstitch** (page 34) on both sides of the bias stem.
► Using #8 EZM14 and a #24 Chenille needle, **Couch** (page 45) in each valley of the small rick-rack in both directions.

Large Leaves:

► Using #8 EZ31 and a #24 Chenille needle, stitch a **Backstitch** (page 34) around the inside layer of each leaf.
► Using #8 EZM14 and a #24 Chenille needle, stitch a **Chain Stitch** (page 169) around the outside of each leaf.

Small Leaves:

► Using #8 EZM14 stitch a **Palestrina Knot** (page 68) for the stem connecting the small leaves.
► With a #24 Chenille needle using #8 EZ31 and #8 EZM21, randomly stitch a **Backstitch** (page 34) around all the small leaves.
► Using #8 EZ31 and a #24 Chenille needle, stitch a **Closed Fly Stitch** (page 58) down the center of three leaves.
► On the three other leaves sew a tiny green button to the center.

Vase:

► Using #8 EZM20 and a #24 Chenille needle, stitch a **Chain Stitch** (page 169) around the vase.
► This is a fun exercise using a **Threaded Backstitch** (page 37) and a **Pekinese Stitch** (page 40) using different weight threads.
► Draw nine horizontal chalk lines on your vase.
► Stitch rows of **Backstitches** (page 34) on these lines using your different weight aqua threads, making sure the first two rows on the upper portion of the vase line up with each other.
► Using your different weights of aqua threads weave the following stitches through your Backstitch rows.

Row	Stitch
1 & 2	Threaded Backstitch
3	Threaded Backstitch
4	Threaded Backstitch
5	Pekinese Stitch
6	Threaded Backstitch
7	Pekinese Stitch
8	Threaded Backstitch
9	Threaded Backstitch

Appliqué:

Cut a 9" piece of the large chartreuse rick rack, chartreuse novelty ribbon and triangular novelty ribbon. Machine sew these vertically to the back (C) starting 1" from the left hand side and making sure the rick-rack is placed under the chartreuse novelty ribbon so that only half of the rick rack shows. Hand sew the tiny red buttons on the top of each hill of the rick-rack.

Cover Assembly (D), (E), & (F):

Pocket:

Fold the Aqua/yellow polka dot pocket (E) in half so that it measures 5-½" x 5-¼". Sew the charcoal cotton print (F) a ½" down from the folded edge of the pocket using a ¼" seam allowance. Sew the Grey circular novelty ribbon in the center of the charcoal overlay. Pin the pocket to the base of (D) and baste in place.

Assembly of Outside:

Sew the outside pieces together in the following order (A) to (C) and then to (D) using a ¼" seam allowance. Using 505™ spray, baste the batting to the back of the outside cover. With your sewing machine sew three vertical lines in the pocket large enough to hold pencils and a ruler.

▶ Using #8 EZ05 stitch a **Palestrina Knot** (page 68) on the two outside sewing lines and a **Threaded Backstitch** (page 37) on the center sewing line of the pocket.

Interior Assembly:

Cut:
- (H) Turquoise Stripe for lining - 16" x 8 ½" (H)
- (I) Charcoal yarn dye fabric for both zipper pockets - Cut four 5" x 8 ½" (x4)
- Chartreuse wool needle case with pinked edges - 8" x 4 ¼" (x2)
- Batting cut one piece - 16" x 8 ½"

Using 505™ spray, baste the batting to the back of the inside lining (H).

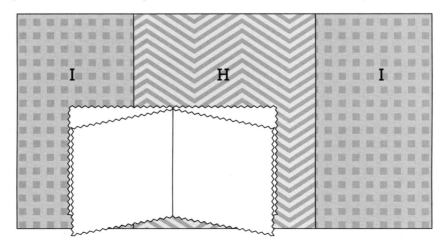

Pocket Assembly:

1) For each pocket (I) make a sandwich by placing the two yarn dyed fabrics (I) right sides together. Sandwich the zipper in the middle making sure your zipper pull starts a ¼" from the edge and that the raw edges of the fabric and the edge of the zipper meet (the zipper will be a little long and will be trimmed to fit the case). Using a zipper foot sew ⅛" from the zipper.

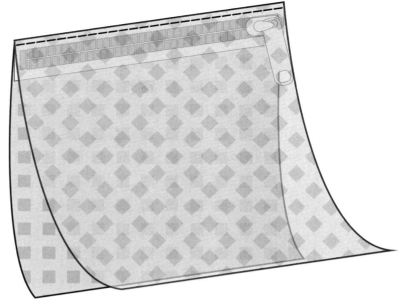

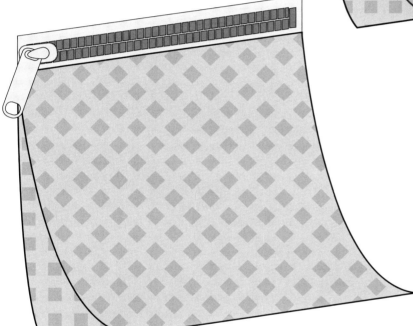

2) Turn your fabrics to the right side and press so that the zipper is exposed.

3) Referring to the illustration, place one pocket on the right hand side and the other on the left hand side of the lining. Baste in place. On each of the pockets sew by machine along the top edge of the zipper a piece of chartreuse novelty ribbon to hide the edge of the zipper.

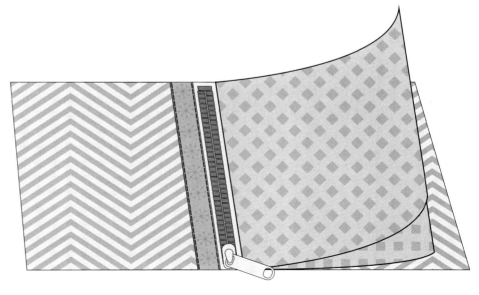

Needle Case:

Make a sandwich by placing the two pinked chartreuse pieces of wool together. Find the center vertical line of the case and pin to the lining making sure you come up ½" from the bottom and center the case on the lining. Sew down the center vertical line to attach your needle case to the lining. Draw a 1-¾" circle on your persimmon wool.

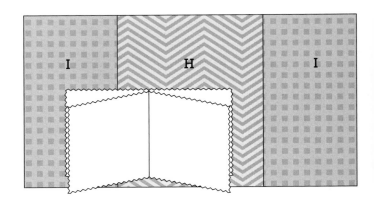

▶ In the center of your circle stitch a Bumble Bee using #5 EZ05 and #5 EZ17 and a #1 Milliners needle for the **Bullion Knot** (page 92) body, #5 EZ05 and a #1 Milliners needle for the **Pistil Stitch** (page 106) antennae and #5 EZ17 for the **Chain Stitch** (page 169) wings.

Cut out the persimmon circle and stitch it to the bottom right hand corner of your needle case.

Hexagon Pincushion:

Make a freezer template of the hexagon. Iron the freezer paper to the persimmon wool and cut out two hexagons. From your orange cotton fabrics cut out and assemble a ½" hexagon using your ½" hexagon papers. Press well and remove the papers. Appliqué the fabric hexagon to the center of your wool hexagon. Cut a ⅝" wool circle and appliqué to the center of your hexagon.

▶ Using #8 EZM36 and a #3 Milliners needle, stitch **Bullion Knots** (page 92) around the center circle.
▶ Using #8 EZM31 and a #24 Chenille needle, stitch a **Backstitch** (page 34) around each fabric hexagon.

Place the two wool hexagons right sides together. Sew around the hexagon using a ¼" seam allowance. Slit the back and turn to the right side. Stuff the hexagon with a little stuffing and whipstitch the slit closed. Once you have sewn the binding in place you will attached the pincushion.

Construction of Needle Roll:

Make a sandwich by placing the cover and the lining wrong sides together. Find the center point of the left hand side of the outside and pin and baste the loop in place so that the raw edge of the fabrics are in line with the raw edges of the elastic.

Baste all layers together using a scant ¼" seam allowance. Cut your striped binding into two 2" strips. Join these on the bias and press the binding in half to make a double binding. On the outside of the needle roll bind the edge using the double binding then hand stitch the binding to the inside of the roll.

Hand stitch the hexagon pincushion in place and sew the button in place to form your closure.

Fill with your favorite sewing supplies!

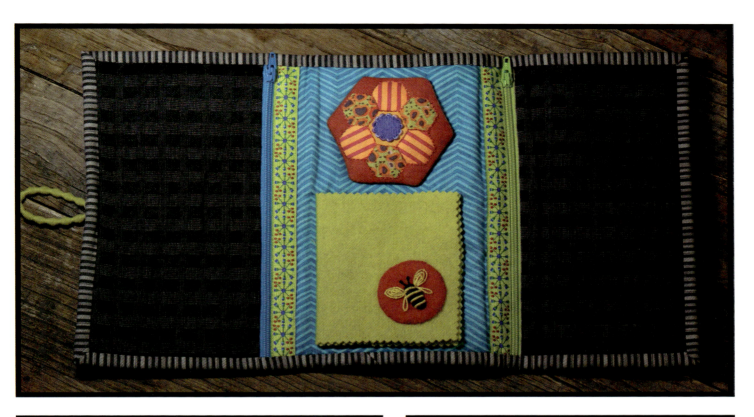

The Fresh Cut Sewing Box

Block Size: 8-½" x 8-¾"

Appliqué Threads:

Ellana Wool Thread:
EN07 Oceanfront
EN09 Amazon Green
EN20 Cloud
EN37 Very Berry
EN49 Kumquat

Efina Cotton Thread:
EF08 Turquoise
EF10 Spring Leaf
EF12 Avocado
EF30 Black
EF43 Dark Cerise

Embellishment Threads:

Eleganza Perle Cotton:

#8 EZ34 Tree Frog
#8 EZM19 Island Oasis
#8 EZM20 Riptide
#5 EZM34 Flutter-by
#3 EZ10 Paradise Blue

Background Fabrics:

Hand Dyed Wools:
Check Black Wool • 8-½" x 8-¾"

Cottons Layering:
Black & White Dot • 2-½" x 5"

Appliqué Fabrics:

Hand Dyed Wools:
Amazon Green • ¾" x 3"
Cloud • ¾" x 5"
Kumquat • 1-¼" x 1-½"
Oceanfront • 4-¾" x 3-¼"
Very Berry • 1-½" x 3-½"

Cottons Fabrics:
Green Stripe • 1-¾" x 7-½"
Pink, Green, & Orange Swirl • 2-½" x 3-¼"
Turquoise & Yellow Dot • 1" x 5"

Additional Materials:

Straps:
Soft & Stable • 2-½" x 11-½"
Black & White Dot Cotton • 6-½" x 12-½"

Bag:
Black Yazzii Deluxe Double Organizer
(Top Handle Removed)

Ribbons:
Green Rick-Rack • 6"
Green & Turquoise Triangle Ribbon • 1-½"

Buttons:
¼" Turquoise Flower • 3 ea
¾" Round Black • 4 ea

Background Assembly:

Background:

Cut: Check Black Wool - 8-½" x 8-¾"

Background Layering:

Cut: Black Polka Dot (x2) - 2-¼" x 1-½" (A and B)
Black Polka Dot - 1-½" x 1-½" (C)

Appliqué the three polka dot pieces to the background referring to the photograph and stitch diagram for placement.

Appliqué:

Stems:

Trace separately with a pencil on the matte side of your freezer paper the vase, leaves and flowers.

For the circles you can either hand cut these using freezer paper templates or use your wool punch. You will need your 1" wool punch for the three large Very Berry berries and your ⅜" punch for the nine Cloud circles and the six Lagoon circles on the leaves.

Cut out each of the freezer paper templates on the pencil line. Referring to the photograph iron the templates to the appropriate color wool and cotton fabrics. The shiny side of your freezer paper is ironed to the right side of all your fabrics.

Remember to cut out the wool appliqué pieces exactly the same size as the template and add a

¼" seam allowance for the cotton appliqué pieces so you can needle turn the fabrics.

Using your small appliqué pins and referring to the diagram pin the ribbon stems and appliqué pieces in place.

Sew the stems in place using cotton thread.

Appliqué the wool pieces using a small whipstitch. I stitch with a #24 Chenille needle using a wool thread that matches the wool color I am appliquéing down.

Next appliqué the cotton fabrics using cotton thread and a #11 Straw needle or #11 Short Darner.

The six Lagoon circles will be whipstitched down after the leaves have been appliquéd down.

Cut a 4-¾" x ¾" strip from the turquoise polka dot fabric centering three light yellow dots. Appliqué the band ½" down from the top of the vase and sew the three flower buttons in the center of the three dots.

Binding the Block:

Cut the binding strip 2" wide. Iron in half and bind the block with a double binding.

Embellish:

Stems:

▶ Using a #3 Milliners needle and #8 EZ34, stitch six horizontal **Pistil Stitches** (page 106) at the base of the flower, three on either side of the triangle ribbon.
▶ Using a #3 Milliners needle and #8 EZ34, stitch two wrap **French Knots** (page 104) on each hill of the rick rack ribbons.
▶ Using your chalk pencil draw the lines to connect the stems from the circles to the vase on the two leaves and the small stem on the left hand side joining the berry to the rick rack stem.
▶ Using #3 EZ10 as the thread you lay down and #8 EZ34 as the thread you stitch with, **Couch Using Bullion Knots** (page 47) on all chalk lines.

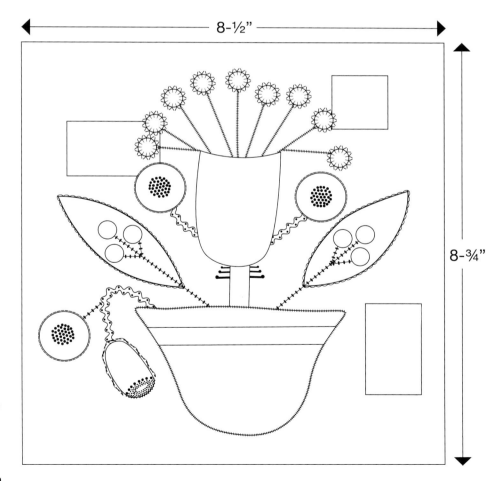

Vase:

► Using #3 EZ10 as the thread you lay down and #8 EZM19 as the thread you stitch with, **Couch** (page 45) around the edge of the vase.

Cloud Dots:

► Using your chalk pencil draw the lines to connect the Cloud dots to the center flower.
► Using #8 EZ34 as the thread you lay down and as the thread you stitch with, **Couch** (page 45) on all chalk lines.
► Using #8 EZM19, stitch a **Fly Stitch** (page 127) around each dot.

Very Berry Berries:

► Using #5 EZM34 and a #1 Milliners needle, stitch a cluster of **French Knots** (page 104) using two wraps in the center of the berries.
► Using #5 EZM34, stitch a **Backstitch** (page 34) around the outer edge of the three berries.

Leaves:

► Using #8 EZ34, stitch a **Chain Stitch** (page 169) around the outer edge of the leaves.

Small Kumquat Flower:

► Using a #3 Milliners needle and #8 EZM20, stitch **French Knots** (page 104) at the base of the flower.
► Using #5 EZM34, stitch a **Threaded Backstitch** (page 37) around the top edge of the flower.
► Using a #1 Milliners needle and #5 EZM34, stitch a row of **French Knots** (page 104) along the top of the turquoise French Knots.

Construction:

Handles:

Cut: Two pieces of Soft and Stable - 11" x 1"
Two Black & White Polka Dot Cotton - 12" x 3"

Iron your two polka dot fabric in half wrong sides together so that they measure 12" x 1-½". Place the soft and stable in the center of the polka dot fabric and fold the seam allowances inwards on all four ends so that the fabric covers the edges of the soft and stable. Pin in place. Machine sew ⅛" in on the four sides of each handle.

Find the center of the sides of the bag and pin the handle in place. Place the inside edges one inch out from the center line with a two inch gap between the handles.

Attach the handles to the bag and finish by stitching a large black button at the base of each handle.

Pin the block to the front of the bag. Hand stitch the block to the bag using a small straight stitch and your black cotton thread.

Carrying Handles:

Cut: Soft and Stable - 18" x 1-¼"
Black & White Dash Cotton - 19" x 4"
Hook & Loop Velcro - 1" Wide x 3" Long

Iron your Black & White Dash Cotton in half wrongs sides together so that they measure 18" x 2". Place the soft and stable in the center of the polka dot fabric and fold the seam allowances inwards on all four ends so that the fabric covers the edges of the soft and stable. Pin in place. Machine sew ⅛" in on the four sides of each handle.

Referring to the diagram below, machine sew the loop Velcro on one end of the handle, flip the handle over and sew the hook Velcro to the opposite end.

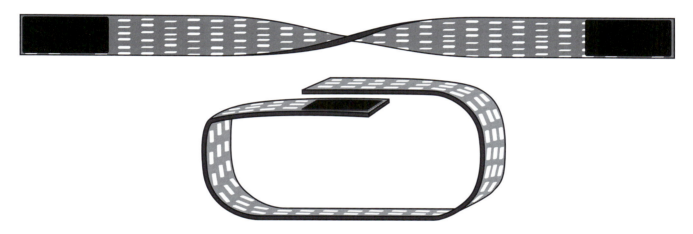

I absolutely love my Fresh Cut Sewing Box. It is the perfect size for the project. Mine is filled with all the threads and notions I need for the blocks.

Creative Stitching,
Sue

STITCH DIAGRAMS

Threaded Double Backstitch

Stitch two rows of Backstitches, making sure your stitches are aligned. Move the working thread through the two rows of Backstitches; moving through the two aligned stitches at the same time. Continue until you reach the final Backstitch.

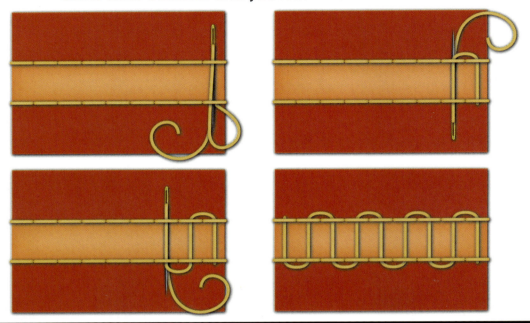

Double Threaded Double Backstitch

Stitch two rows of Backstitches, making sure your stitches are aligned. Move the working thread through the two rows of Backstitches, moving through the two aligned stitches at the same time. Once you reach the end of the backstitches, move to the opposite side and continue weaving until you reach the end.

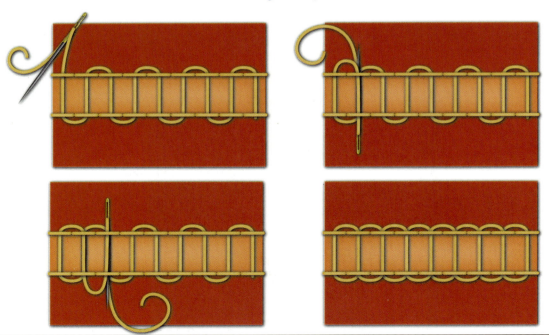

STITCH KEY

Backstitch (page 34)	Italian Knotted Border Stitch (page 62)
Bullion Knot (page 92)	Needle Weave Bar (page 166)
Bullion Rose (page 110)	Open Buttonhole Filler (page 141)
Cast on Bullion Knot (page 164)	Palestrina Knot (page 68)
Chain Stitch (page 169)	Pekinese Stitch (page 40)
Closed Fly Stitch (page 58)	Pistil Stitch (page 106)
Closed Tete de Boeuf (page 135)	Rosette Chain Stitch (page 129)
Couching (page 45)	Running Stitch (page 26)
Couching with Bullion Knots (page 47)	Scroll Stitch (page 133)
Crested Chain Stitch (page 124)	Seed Stitch (page 55)
Cross Stitch	Split Stitch (page 79)
Detached Chain Stitch (page 52)	Star Stitch (page 170)
Double Cast on Stitch (page 96)	Stem Stitch (page 82)
Double Open Buttonhole Filler	Threaded Backstitch (page 37)
Double Threaded Double Backstitch (page 38)	Threaded Double Backstitch (page 37)
Drizzle Stitch (page 100)	Trellis Stitch (page 114)
Eyelet Wheel (page 112)	Van Dyke Stitch (page 87)
Fly Stitch (page 127)	Whipped Backstitch (page 35)
French Knot (page 104)	Whipped Woven Circle (page 120)
Herringbone Stitch (page 168)	Woven Picot (page 148)

CREATIVE IDEAS

Kim Solis
Ukiah, CA
Photos courtesy of Doug Solis

Julie Johnson
Winnetka, IL
Quilted By Anne Books
of Mequon, WI